STUDIES IN INDIAN TEXTILES

(Collection in Salarjung Museum & State Museum, Hyderabad)

STUDIES IN INDIAN TEXTILES

(Collection in Salarjung Museum & State Museum, Hyderabad)

V. SUGUNA SARMA

BKP

BHARATIYA KALA PRAKASHAN

DELHI (INDIA)

First Published 1998

Published by C.P. Gautam
BHARATIYA KALA PRAKASHAN
3611/5, Narang Colony, Tri Nagar,
Delhi-110035 Phone : 7192770

ISBN : 81-86050-13-2

Typesetting at PAU Computers
3421-A, Narang Colony, Tri Nagar,
Delhi-110035 Phone : 7195651

Printed at Santosh Offset
40, Anand Nagar, Inderlok, Delhi
Phone : 511 6763, 511 7390

Dedicated

In Memory of
My Beloved Father
& Mother
(Late) Sri V. Ramanatha Sarma
and
(Late) Smt. V. Jayaprada Devi

CONTENTS

FOREWORD

All human institutions over a time change responding to the needs of the society. Thus Museums which were once considered to be principally "the store-houses" of antiquities for preservation today are conceived as instruments of education and dissemination of knowledge. In this context the study, analysis and publication of the results of Museums objects assume great significance. Dr. Miss V. Suguna Sarma's Ph.D work on Studies in Indian Textiles is a definite contribution in this direction. I heartily congratulate Dr. Suguna and Publisher, Mr. Gautam of Bharatiya Kala Prakashan, for bringing out an important work of this nature and I am sure, the scholars and general public would welcome it.

Indian textiles have gained demand and acquired fame for quality and utility all over the world throughout history. This Indian tradition is continuing to this day. Therefore, textiles are one of the principal components of India's proud heritage which needs to be preserved and continued. Dr. Suguna's book studies the textile collections in the two renowned Museums of the city of Hyderabad i.e., the Salar Jung Museum and the Government of Andhra Pradesh State Museum. These Museum collections comprise a variety of Textile objects belonging to different periods and from different parts of the country and abroad. As such this study would be of interest not only from a regional view-point, but for the other parts of the land. As such there is much scope for the authoress for continuing her study in the line of textile collections in museums.

Dr. Suguna's work is a comprehensive and interesting topic of its kind, dealing with the collection of textiles chosen from the angles of material, technique of production, colours and designs and its utility. Since she is working for the Archaeology and Museums department, dealing with museum materials, the study emphasis with the relevant technical aspects of Museology. There is thus, a separate chapter on "Storage and Preservation".

Architecture, Cuisine and Textiles are important aspects of mankind and obviously create interest to all. I am sure this well-written, carefully printed and adequately illustrated publication will be appreciated by everyone who reads it.

M. RADHAKRISHNA SARMA
(Retd) Professor and Head
Department of Ancient Indian History
Culture and Archaeology
Osmania University, Hyderabad

PREFACE

In this book, an attempt has been made to study the Textile objects in the two reputed museums of Hyderabad City viz., the Salar Jung Museum and the State Museum, Hyderabad. Museum collections consist of a variety of Textile objects belonging to different periods and from different parts of the country and abroad. But generally, only 1/4 of the total collections of objects in a museum are on display while the rest of the objects are preserved as Reserve Collections in the stores. The few objects exhibited are only noticed, while the reserve collections as in the case of State Museum, Hyderabad, whose textiles are not displayed, are hardly known to people excepting to a few experts and scholars who may know them. As such there is a need to bring to light the different aspects and details of those objects in the collections of museums under study.

Old specimens of Textiles are becoming rare and fading away with time. In the present generation, very few museums are having a truly good collection of these organic objects. Thus, a need is felt for the layman and the scholar a-like in the contemporary time to know the glorious tradition of textile art through the museum collection.

The book is conceived in seven chapters.

The work begins with a *Prologue* in which a general background of the Origin of Textiles is given with special reference to the earliest evidences of textiles in Andhra Pradesh.

A *Descriptive Catalogue of Textiles* in the two museums under study is made in the second chapter of the book.

The third chapter is related to the *Fabrics* in which the textiles are classified into different fabric materials viz., cotton, silk, woollen and mixed fabrics. The nature of different fabric materials are studied in a detailed manner in relation to the textiles under study.

The fourth chapter deals with the *Technique* employed in manufacturing the various types of textiles and their sub-varieties.

The fifth chapter is devoted to the *Colour and Design*. In this the colour scheme, designs and patterns are studied.

The *Utility* of each textile specimen in possession of the two museums under study is dealt in the Sixth Chapter.

Since the present work relates to the textiles collection from the museums, it would be desirable to study in brief the problems arising out of storage and preservation of these organic materials. Hence, the seventh chapter gives a brief account of the *Storage and Preservation* of textiles and costumes in museum atmosphere.

The textile collection from the two museums under study are arranged in a tabular form at the end.

Appendix A - Textile collection from the Salar Jung Museum, Hyderabad.

Appendix B - Textile collection from the State Museum, Hyderabad.

In this connection, I wish to express my indebtedness to all distinguished scholars from whose works relevant materials have been drawn and incorporated in this book and also various individuals and institutions who helped me in the completion of this work.

I express my profound gratitude of Prof. M. Radhakrishna Sarma, former Professor and Head of the Department, Ancient Indian History, Culture and Archaeology, Osmania University, for his valuable suggestions and excellent guidance at all stages of the work, which enabled me to bring this work to completion.

This work, being a modified version of my doctoral thesis written under the supervision of Prof. S. Dhareshwari, Professor, Department of Ancient Indian History, Culture and Archaeology, Osmania University, who with great affection, guided me and helped me with precious suggestions. For which I express my thanks to her and also the Osmania University authorities for giving me this opportunity to pursue research work and publish the same (Lr. No. 265/DA/1993).

I gratefully acknowledge the help I received from the former Director Dr. M.L. Nigam and the staff of Salar Jung Museum for allowing access to the relevant data available in the museum.

I like to extend my gratitude to Sri. N.R.V. Prasad and to Dr. V.V. Krishna Sastry, Former Directors, State Archaeology and Museums Department, Andhra Pradesh for permitting me to make use of the materials available in the State Museum, Hyderabad relating to my research topic; my thanks are due to Sri Jogi Naidu, Curator, State Museum, Hyderabad and also to Sri V.V.S. Avadhani and Late Sri S. Ramakantham, Former Curators.

I also record my thanks to Dr. N.S. Ramachandra Murthy, Assistant Director (Publication), Sri M.A. Qaiyyum, Assistant Director (Conservation), Dr. B. Subrahmanyam, Research and Training Officer; Sri. P. Vengal Reddy, Dr. K. Padmanabha and Dr. E. Siva Nagi Reddy, Technical Assistants and also Smt. B. Indumathi Devi, Publication Assistant for their kind help and valuable suggestions.

I am extremely thankful to Mrs. Dorothy, former I/C Librarian, Osmania University, Sri P. Ramesh, Librarian, Salar Jung Museum, Smt. M. Varalaxmi, Gazetted Librarian, State Archaeology and Museums, Andhra Pradesh and to the Librarian, State Archives, Andhra Pradesh for extending me Library facilities.

I also extended my gratitude to the Photography Section of the Salar Jung Museum and the Department of Archaeology and Museums, Andhra Pradesh, Hyderabad.

I express my grateful thanks to Sri D. Gnaneswar who took great care in typing the work very neatly in a short time.

My thanks are due to Sri V.K. Sushil Kumar, Director, Anish Computer Services, Safilguda for taking great care and interest in bringing out the printouts with great care and diligence.

I express my indebted gratitude to my mother late Smt. V. Jayaprada Devi for her encouragement and support in my research work. I, therefore, deeply regret that she had not lived long enough to bless me for the publication of this study which, I in all reverence and humility dedicate to her. My special thanks are to all my family members who rendered their co-operation to bring this work to completion. In this connection my sincere thanks are due to all my friends who helped me with their valuable suggestions and encouragement.

Finally, I wish to thank Sri P.C. Gautam of Bharatiya Kala Prakashan, New Delhi for publishing this work in an impressive manner.

V. SUGUNA SARMA

15th Aug, 1997
Hyderabad

LIST OF PLATES

A. PLATES (Black and White)

B. PLATES (Colour)

CHAPTER - I

PROLOGUE

Antiquity of Textiles

It is evidently observed that very little attention has been paid by eminent scholars and Historians to work on the subject from research point of view, particularly no comprehensive and exhaustive study has been made on the Historical back-ground of Textiles from Andhra Pradesh in a systematic way. It is felt necessary to study the antiquity of the costumes and textiles in Andhra Pradesh and also the materials employed, basing on the Paintings, Sculptural, Inscriptional and Literary sources available. Study of objects displayed in the Salar Jung Museum and State Museum, at Hyderabad show the textile design and weaving techniques, embroidery and other aspects relating to textiles, not only from Andhra Pradesh but also from different regions of our country for a comparative study. These Museums possess plenty of first hand material. Further, study of sculptural panels right from early historic to the modern period may give the various developmental stages, occurred from time to time and also study of contemporary Literature and Accounts of Foreign travellers provide the style and fashion of costumes and the use of various materials in those days.

Hence, this attempt may help to trace the antiquity of Textiles and different materials like cotton, silk, woollen etc., probable centres to manufacture the textiles and also to locate the trading centres in Andhra Pradesh.

The Earliest Evidences

The Pre-Historic Age of Andhra Pradesh remains a mystery as far as our subject under study is concerned. Because there are no authenticated evidences available to clinch our problem. It remains a dark age of the World of textiles.

A good number of Rock-art places datable to Upper Palaeolithic or Mesolithic period have been discovered in Andhra Pradesh. None of these have shown wearing a simple cover to the body or covering private parts of the body. For example, generally the rock paintings represented with linear drawings of men holding weapons specially in hunting scenes, exhibited prominently the genital portion of the male figurines which clearly suggest the absence of wearing protective materials for the body.

There is clear indication to nudity during the upper Palaeolithic Age. A group of paintings were discovered in the rock shelters near Ketavaram. The paintings, all of red ochre, are noticed over the front portion of the overhanging rock shelters and natural caverns. The principal theme depicted is the jungle life. We find a number of little men, shown in perspective, scaling a hill, or a man with his genitals prominently shown, stood up in horror and raised his arms for the help at the sight of a tiger. There is a head of a tribal chief wearing a diadem. These examples clearly indicate the absence of wearing drapery during the upper Palaeolithic period.

In Megalithic context an incised drawing of a deceased human figure packed probably with the help of wild reeds was noticed on one of the orthostats of an oblong cist burial at Chinnamaruru in Mahbubnagar district of Andhra Pradesh. Here, incised drawing of a human is seen on the western orthostat of the cist. The stylized human form executed on the orthostat is in the horizontal form, in double line, unlike those found in cave paintings which are single lined and painted in various hues. The figure is formed by drawing two oblique lines, diagonally, crossing each other to form two triangles. The inverted one occurring on the top represents the torso and the everted one stands for the lower part and shows the pelvic region. The everted triangle is further sub-divided into two unequal wide triangular projections as if to suggest legs, facing different directions. On the top of the inverted triangle is shown a circle suggesting the head without any details. Similarly hands are shown in conventional pattern depicting them as ropes suspended from either end of the angle with ends curved. A starting line in the middle is drawn from the point of neck to the legs and hatchings executed thinly in either direction suggesting the figure is dressed. This was the first example to report or to know the way of dressing the deceased person.

Discovery of spindle-whorls from Nagarjunakonda suggests the knowledge of weaving technology. The discovery of needles made of bone at Chinnamarur in Chalcolithic levels suggests some sort of primitive type of stitching leather for different purposes.

Terracottas

Terracotta figures were found in large numbers belonging to Mauryan and Satavahana levels. A study of these figures not only reveal the artistic nature of the people but also their social, cultural and economic background. The figures are noticed at Yeleswaram, Nagarjunakonda, Nelakondapalle, Dhulikatta and Peddabankur etc., all prominent Buddhist sites. The terracottas manufactured here were exported to other places.

A terracotta figurine from the village Vanitamandalam is an unique example found from the Mauryan levels. Vanitamandalam is situated on the northern bank of River Vamsadhara opposite to the famous Buddhist site, Salihundam, 19 kms. from Srikakulam.[1] The figure is that of a *dancing girl.* She is seen wearing a jacket of sleeveless variety, decorated with a border of beaded design at the bottom. She wears a short-skirt with winged extensions as her lower garment. It is further treated with vertical folds, the ends of which skillfully decorated with embossed flowers, finished with a line of beads, running horizontally from one end to another. The head is decorated with a scarf having a richly decorated border pinned with rattles.

The position of hands, the hair-style and costumes definitely suggest that the figure is a dancing girl.[2] The fluttering skirt at the sides, and the way of tightening of hair with a scarf indicates, the swift movement of the dance. The style of hair dress and the costumes she has worn reminds us the present day Manipuri dancers. There is no doubt that this dress is not of local character, and may suggest an alien contact with the region. It may also be an Iranian influence especially in hair style and dress. The figure is a master-piece of terracotta art and a rare specimen so far discovered in the region.

Archaic terracottas were found at Peddabankur in large numbers in the Mauryan and Satavahana levels.[3] They comprise human and animal figurines. The heads of many figures are broken.

Male figures - This type consists of crudely made figures of male deity with hands and legs shown as tapering masses, pinched nose and eye sockets filled in with applique eye balls. The head tapers to a point and has a prominent band at the top. The waist-band is shown with incisions. The second figure is also a male figure (deity) with similar hands and legs and with feet curved forward.[4]

From the above description we can assume that probably a turban was worn on the head. Obviously, there is a clear evidence of a waist-band.

Among the other Peddabankur figures, there is a kaolin figure of a boy with a turban-like head-dress.[5] The figure is devoid of any ornamentation. As such, it may be the representation of a commoner boy of the early historic period.

The figure of *Mother and Child,* found in the Yeleswaram Excavation is 11 cms. long, without head and feet, both being mutilated and missing.[6] The child in her arms is 6 cms. long. Here, the mother is seen wearing an undergarment, the folds of which are visible in the middle of her legs. No blouse is depicted.

On stylistic grounds and also according to the level in which the figure was found at Yeleswaram excavation, it is datable to 3rd century A.D.[7] In most of the Satavahana and Ikshvaku sculptures we find the undergarment with a knot over the navel and the folds in the middle run down to the knees.

Costumes as gleaned through the Sculptures

The following study is based on the hypothesis of the sculptors who depicted the sculptures and reliefs, had their mind on the contemporary persons and things around them. Although, they provided the figures in accordance with the requirements of the texts and also with those occurrings in their society and environment. So, many of the items found in the sculptures may be indigenous to the land they belong to and its surrounding region formed a part. Therefore, the sculptural art preserves for us the reflections of the various aspects of contemporary life, along with the types of dresses, which compose a particular culture.

Literature is not of great help for the history of costume in this period. In Buddhist texts, literary references to costume are scrappy, and the words used for certain pieces of apparel or certain kinds of material are passed over without further comment. At this juncture, fortunately, the reliefs of Amaravati come to our rescue in clinching our problem of study to some extent.

Dhanakataka, modern Amaravati, emerged as the most prolific centre of Buddhism[8]. All the architectural fragments of Amaravati have been divided into four periods, ranging from 300 B.C. to 350 A.D.[9] Every period shows its own type of human anatomy, dress, ornaments, poses and grouping. The technique of story-telling in bas-relief which was evolved at Barhut, has gained maturity at Sanchi and perfected at Amaravati during the reign of the Satavahanas.[10]

The main article in the costume of the male figures is dhoti, which reaches down the knees, one end of which is tucked at the back and the other gathered in folds and tucked in the front. (Fig.12)[11] or rarely, one end is tied round the waist and the other taken over the left elbow and let fall down (Fig.13)[12] The dhoti is secured to the waist with a kamarband with bow-shaped knot. The upper part of the body is usually represented bare except for the scarf.[13]

All the male figures wear a turban. It seems that the long turban scarf was twisted with hair braids to obtain many beautiful forms. The commonest variety is found in Barhut fashion - the hair is gathered in top-knot, one end of the scarf is made to cover it, and then three or more rounds (Fig.14)[14].

Turban - The variation of the same form may be seen in these figures. The forms being obtained by arranging the top-knot either pearshaped or elliptical. In another variety, some part of the scarf seems to have been rolled and kept in straight line with the top-knot; then several rounds were wound and finally the end was passed through the folds, taken over the rolled part and tucked to the side. (Figs. 15, 16, 17, 18, 19)[15] Caps - The caps may also be seen in the scene depicting stupa worship by foreigners. (Figs. 31 and 32)[16].

The women during the Satavahana age, are represented wearing two types of lower garments. One is "langoti" in which one end of a narrow scarf is attached to the waist-girdle and the other tucked behind. (Fig.40)[17] In the second variety one end of the loin cloth reaching to the knees is wrapped round the waist and the other end is pleated and tucked in front and passed through the loins and tucked behind. (Figs. 41 and 42)[18], Here the loin cloth is wrapped round the waist and the pleated end tucked at the side. Some times the kamarband was also worn. The women occasionally wore turbans. (Fig. 43)[19].

For example, the following are a few evidences from *Amaravati Sculptures* which denote the dress of the individual belonging to different sections of the contemporary society:

The dress of the *king* and his *queens* gleaned through a sculptured panel. This sculptured slab shows the figures of man of rank, perhaps a king and two women, evidently his queens standing on a platform. The apparel is striped and transparent, its texture being suggested by working it closely on the body, but the tassels are heavy and elaborate as also the waistline. Though draped the women are essentially nude as in Kushan a sculptures from Mathura (Pl .xxiii, Fig.2)[20].

The dress of a group of *devotees* can be seen on a slab of the stupa. This sculptured slab depicts the dress of devotees, who are naked upto the waist wearing waist-bands with the knots tied at the side of the waist. All the devotees are seen wearing a turban (Pl. xxxix, Fig.2)[21].

Another sculptured slab depicts the dress of a *snakecharmer*. He is seen wearing a waist-band and a lower garment. No turban is seen on the head (Pl .xxxvi, Fig.1)[22].

On one of the slabs, the dress of foreigners is depicted. In this scene, the messengers from some foreign country are shown. It is noticeable that the strangers are fully clothed in tunic upto the ankles (Pl. xxv, Fig. 2)[23].

The Andhras also seem to have understood the importance of a uniform for *soldiers*, as fighting in dhoti and long flowing dupattas must have hindered action. In this period we find soldiers dressed in tunics and kilts and turbans (Figs. 60, 61)[24].

Among the literary evidences of the history of textiles and costumes we have one *literary* work of the Satavahana period, i.e., the poetical composition written by Hala, *Gathasaptasati* in Prakrit. It contains some interesting references to dress. It appears that, most of the women were sparsely dressed. In some of the verses Hala mentions that women covered their upper part of their body with a blue bodice or a blue robe. There are references to silk cloths and silken garments. The poet also refers to dyed cloth, yellow coloured garments etc. In another verse Hala refers to a needle, perhaps the art of stitching was also in vogue, however there are no references to the art of tailoring and stitching of cut garments.

The Sculptures from Nagarjunakonda and Goli belong to the Ikshvaku period. The art of Nagarjunakonda, as Sarkar has suggested, is divided into two phases : earlier phase belonging to the time of Virapurusadatta and the other to the time of Ehuvala Chamtamula.[25]

The exotic atmosphere that pervaded the Krishna Valley is best evidenced in the art of Nagarjunakonda. Certain alterations in Indo-Scythian costume are seen in the Nagarjunakonda sculptures.[26] The sculptural art of the Ikshvaku period during the third century A.D. was rich and sufficient. Evidence has survived at Goli, Amaravati, Uppugunduru, Chandavaram, Gummadidurru, Guntupalli, Nelakondapalli, Alluru, Salihundam etc.[27]

Most of the Buddha figures at Goli show preference to the robe covering both shoulders. The treatment of Sanghati is fluid and wavy; large folds flowing in linear fashion characterise the Buddha figures. The garment is often shown in Greco-Roman fashion.[28]

A majestic figure of standing Buddha at Alluru shows the right shoulder uncovered and the prominent pleats of the robe rendered artistically.[29]

Besides, the bas-reliefs from Nagarjunakonda, the Goli reliefs are important documents to study the history of costumes in Southern India, had not undergone any considerable change since the earlier days of the Satavahana rule at Amaravati and Nagarjunakonda.

Nagarjunakonda and Goli Reliefs : The costumes worn by different individuals :

The apparel of the Kings represented in the Nagarjunakonda reliefs is very scanty. It is surprising that the king represented in the Nagarjunakonda sculptures is almost bare bodied except for his lower garment, a langoti and an occasional upper garment *(uttariya)*. Perhaps the scantiness of dress in sculptures was necessitated, as construed by Rajendralal Mitra, owing to the exigencies of art; or it might be that the persons sculptured in the reliefs of Nagarjunakonda wore a diaphanous costume.[30] However, among the aristocratic persons depicted in the sculptures of Nagarjunakonda, the king is shown wearing a few items of dress. For example, we may see the dress worn by a king in the different panels :

In this panel, besides the usual lower garment and a waist band, the king is seen wearing a rolled scarf round his neck *(uttariya)* and a long strip of cloth slings from his waist-band in between his legs. The rolled scarf is folded in the middle by gathering the two ends together and then worn, the loop and the ends falling back over the shoulders. The upper garment is usually seen as a single piece of cloth of considerable length. At times the upper cloth was ornamented with precious stones forming lovely borders. Some of the Amaravati reliefs reveal such borders. (Longhurst Pl.XXX-C).[31]

This panel depicts a new kind of dress for the Chakravartin. He wears a tight pyjama or trouser. A large piece of cloth serving as a waist-band holds it in position under which is worn a girdle of string beads. A larger loop hangs down from the knot which comes on the left hip, and a strip of cloth hangs between the legs from the centre of the girdle. No upper garment is seen. (Longhurst, PL.XXX-6).[32]

In the representation of *Gods and Goddesses*, the Hindu and Buddhist art shows, marked reliance on the prevailing fashions in the upper classes. We find Gods wearing the same dresses as the kings. In a panel a host of gods are seen seated around Buddha's throne. In this, all of them are seen wearing langotis, tied to the waist by a waist-band, its ends hang on one side and the loops on the other. But only Indra is represented as wearing a cap or a cylindrical turban. He is seen wearing a long dhoti reaching upto his ankles and also an uttariya on his upper body.[33]

Goddesses and *Celestial beings* represented in the bas-reliefs wear apparel exactly similar to that of the queens. They are shown scantily dressed and their costume includes only a langoti in a majority of cases.

The bas-reliefs from Nagarjunakonda disclose *royal ladies* in a scanty dress and divulge no dissimilarity of dress when compared to the ladies of the lower classes. In majority of the cases, scantily clad *queens* appear wearing a solitary langoti which is usually decorated with its knot shown in the front. But in some cases waist-bands are seen tied over the lower-garments with their knots and projecting loops on the sides.[34] But there is only one panel in which the queen is shown clad in a different style. Here, the queen is shown clad in a sari or dhoti, she wears it round her loins, reaching upto her knees. However, her upper portion is bare. (Fig. IV-14).[35]

In a panel depicting *Ghata Jataka,* shows *Prince* Upasagara as attired in the most decent dress befitting his position. He is seen wearing a tunic which is round at the neck and has long sleeves. It is secured at the waist with a scarf to which is attached a sword. An upper-garment is worn which while passing across the body, coils round the left shoulder and falls back. (Fig. III-8)[36].

On one of the slabs of Goli stupa is portrayed a standing figure of *Prince* Siddhartha. Unfortunately the slab is broken and is in four pieces. Here, the Prince is shown wearing a lower-garment extending upto the ankles. The folds of which are clearly seen. The garment is secured at the waist with a waist-band with a side knot and a central tassel. (Pl. IX-Fig.16).[37]

The *Princesses* illustrated in the bas-reliefs are meagerly dressed. They resemble those worn by the queens. One of the panels show a princess wearing a different attire, she appears to wear a sari covering her entire body, exactly in the same manner as we see in the present-day style of sari-wearing. (Fig. IV-16)[38].

A panel depicting Dasaratha Jataka shows Princess Sita attired in a different manner. She wears a piece of cloth round her loins without any waist-band or any upper-garment. Here, the sari or the dhoti worn round the waist is above the knees. (Fig. IV-17)[39].

Pairs of Human figures depicted on the various slabs in the vertical panels are termed as "Amorous Couples" by Longhurst. These pairs represent persons of nobility or royalty, as can be seen from their dress. The male is depicted in the same dress as that of a king. A langoti with a kamarband over it, the ends of which are left hanging down or floating, and a piece of cloth tucked in it at the sides or behind. To this sometimes was added an uttariya (Fig. III, 3, 4, Goli - Pls. ' B; IV)[40]. The female dress in the amorous couples resembles that seen on the queens. They are represented almost bare-bodied except for the use of a lower garment at times tied with a waist-band and occasionally an upper-garment is seen. (Fig. IV-15)[41].

The dress of the *dwarfs* consist of a short dhoti which ends well above the knee and is secured at the waist by a waist-band. (Fig. III, 10)[42]. One of the panels show an *udarabandha* in addition to his short dhoti. It is tied round his stomach with its knot on the right side. The loop and tassels of which are quite clear. (Longhurst IX-)[43].

The *ministers* depicted in the Nagarjunakonda sculptures are well dressed in contrast to the sparsely dressed kings. In one of the panels, a minister is shown wearing a close fitting tunic having sleeves down to the wrists. The neck of the garment is round; a waist-band is tied round the waist and a sword is attached to it. A scarf passes round the waist and from, over the left shoulder falls on the back. The body below the waist is shown covered with a dhoti or a loin-cloth which reaches up the ankle. (Longhurst Pl.xxv-a)[44]. In another panel, a minister is seen wearing a pyjama or trousers and an upper garment (Fig.III, 11)[45]. The pyjamas worn by the ministers could be of central Asian origin. According to Mc.Covern, for centuries, wearing of trousers was confined exclusively to the inhabitants of central Asia and this custom spread to all parts of the globe[46].

The *soldiers* depicted in the Nagarjunakonda sculptures may be classified into foreign and local on account of the dress they wear. The foreign soldiers distinguish themselves with their dresses which are altogether different and alien to the native ones[47]. On one of the carved pillars of the palace is seen a bearded soldier, obviously, he is a Scythian warrior. He is shown wearing a helmet, a quilted full-sleeved coat or a tunic and tight fitting trousers; he is seen holding a heavy spear. This full sleeved coat is essentially a central Asian garment which possibly came to India with Scythians in the Kushan period (Fig.IV, 18)[48]. On another panel, a soldier is seen wearing a half sleeved tunic and a helmet (Fig.III, 19)[49]. His lower-garment is not clearly visible. This half-sleeved tunic is a new introduction, once again of central Asian origin, according to Dr. Agarwala. He says that some men are shown wearing it in the earlier group of paintings at Ajanta and in the reliefs of Sanchi. In one panel a soldier is seen wearing a loose-cloak secured at the neck. Agarwala identifies this cloak as an *'achchhadanka'* which is referred to in the *Harsacarita*. We have only a few delineated examples of native soldiers, in the reliefs. Their dress is similar to that of the royal attendants. They are shown wearing a langoti over which is tied a waist-band (Longhurst, Pl.XLVIII-a)[50].

The chauri-bearers are rendered with great delight in the reliefs at Nagarjunakonda. Both *male* and *female* chauri bearers appear. The female chauri-bearer's costume is scanty and akin to that of the queens and princesses. The dress includes a decorated lower-garment with a vastragranthi in the front and occasionally a waist-band tied round the loins. In no case an upper-garment is worn. (Longhurst Pl.XII-a)[51]. Regarding the dress of the male chauri-bearers the reliefs do not offer much information. There is only one example where the royalty is shown attended by a male chauri-bearer. His dress is exactly similar to that of the kings. No upper garment is worn[52]. Similar dress is worn by *fan bearers; umbrella bearers; the standard bearers; the sword bearers; door keepers etc.*

The portrayal of the *Kancukis* in sculptures of Amaravati and Nagarjunakonda is common. In ancient Sanskrit literature he is always described as an old man clad in white clothes, moving about in the harem and palaces with the help of his long staff which is the sign of his oldage. A panel depicts an old man, resembling the *Kancuki*. Here, unfortunately, the long tunic which the *Kancuki* generally wears cannot be made out (Longhurst - Pl-XXXIV-b)[53]. Representation of *Buddhist monks* abound in the sculptures of Nagarjunakonda. The monks are shown wearing a long dhoti, reaching the ankles, (worn in the Vikaccha fashion) with an upper garment. A full view of the monk's dress is revealed in one of the panels. (Longhurst, Pl. XLVIII-b). Here a group of monks who offer comprehensive view of their dress is depicted. (Fig. IV, 21)[54].

The dress of a *dancer* comprised of a dhoti or loin-cloth generally reaching a little above the ankles secured by a kamarband and whose ends are tucked and looped at the sides of the waist. In dancing these looped ends added movement to the simple costume of the dancer. (Fig.87; Longhurst, Pl.XXII, A)[55].

From the material available, there is hardly any disparity between the higher and lower classes, either in the articles of dress or in the mode of wearing them.

An idea about the attire of the *Brahmins* can be had from one of the panels illustrating the *Vessantara Jataka* from Goli[56]. It is interesting to note that the brahmins here are dressed much in the same way as modern orthodox brahmins are in the Telugu and Tamil Countries and that one of them has got his upper cloth tied in the *yajnopavita* fashion, a typically brahminical mode. In general, the dress of a brahmin consisted of a langoti - at times secured by a waist-band and an upper garment[57].

The *Mahauts* wore simple dress which comprised of a langoti - at times fastened by a waist-band. He also wore a cap. The lower class *grooms* are said to have worn a tunic over a langoti. An ideal representation of this class is delineated in Channa the groom and the charioteer of prince Siddhartha. His dress consists of a short-tailored shirt resembling a Roman tunic. (Longhurst, Fig. XIX-b, XXII-b)[58].

The *Pilgrims* - dress comprised of a short dhoti with a uttariya on the top (Longhurst, Pl.XXXI-C, Fig.III,2)[59].

The *Villagers* are shown wearing short dhotis extending upon the knees. A waist-band is tied round the waist. There is no upper garment. (Ramachandra, Pl.XXX-b)[60].

The dress of *Children* is represented in one of the panels at Goli. (Plate II F)[61]. Here, one of the boys who holds a water vessel is dressed resembling the Tamilian and Telugu way of dressing of boys to-day. Here, the boys are seen naked upto the waist except for a waist cloth with folds hanging in front.

Reliefs from Amaravati, Nagarjunakonda and Goli serve ample material in the sculptures of the Satavahana and Ikshvaku periods for reconstruction of the history of Textiles and costumes of Andhradesa. The reliefs from these places besides furnishing details of the typical costumes worn by people belonging to different classes of the contemporary society, also give ample information about the local fashions in the mode of wearing dhotis and saris etc.

The costumes worn by men, women and children was extremely simple during the Satavahana and Ikshavaku times. Generally, it consisted of loin-cloths of very fine material and Kamarbands were worn in different styles. The tunic was worn by soldiers, hunters and guards at the palace gate; the use of caps was in vogue.

As in the case of the Satavahana period, the literature of the Ikshvaku period too, is not very helpful in giving information about the costumes of the people.

The Vishnukundins ruled from 375 A.D. The founder of this dynasty was Indravarman. Their early activity was centered around Nalgonda - Mahbubnagar districts[62]. The products of Brahmanical art-tradition flourished during the Vishnukundin rule. At Chejerla few early sculptures are preserved in the precincts of the Kapoteswara temple. The Surya, a lime stone panel of 5th century A.D. can be regarded as the earliest in Andhradesa. Here, Surya is seen standing holding a lotus by the stem in each uplifted hand. He is dressed in tunic and a flowing under garment. He wears a tall crown, an *Yajnopavita* etc. The folds of the undergarment is secured at the waist into a knot from which the folds fall in a straight manner and the rippling effect is shown in vertical striation[63].

Early Medieval and Medieval Periods

From the 6th century to the middle of the 8th century, a great empire of the Chalukyas ruled the entire Deccan comprising Karnataka and Andhra. A new style of Brahmanical art form was established. The temples situated at Alampur, Kudavali, Panyam, Mahanandi and Satyavolu belong to this style[64]. The temples were adorned with sculptures of numerous Hindu Gods and Goddesses, scenes carved from Hindu Mythology and other celestial Beings. However, there is no change in the style of wearing costumes by the individuals, irrespective of class or caste. They are seen almost in the same attire as was seen in the early reliefs of Amaravati, Nagarjunakonda and Goli.

The following are a few examples of drapery as gleaned through the sculptures from Brahmanical art-tradition:

1. A temple at Kudavali portrays the sculpture of *Harihara*, standing rigidly in a niche. This heavy hour-glass shaped torso is adorned with a simple beaded *hara* and a studded *yajnopavita*. The *Kativastra* reaches the ankle with billowing folds at the waist, and the sash falls in front in circular fashion. (The Sangameswara Temple Kudavali)[65].
2. In another panel, *Siva* is seen wearing a ratna *udarabandha* and *katibandha*. He is seen wearing only a short *Kativastra.* (pl. 54, p.81)[66].
3. In a different temple, at the same place, Siva-Dakshinamurti is seen in seated posture. He is seen attired in a *short pleated Kativastra.* (pl. 65, p.96)[67].

After the *Gathasaptasati* of the Satavahana period, we have ample literary evidence for the period of the Chalukyas of Kalyana. Somesvara, the Western Chalukya king who ruled from A.D. 1124-1138, in his encyclopaedic work, *Manasollasa*, gives details of costumes and textiles common in Karnataka and all over India[68].

It is said that the medieval Indian *Kings* changed their garments according to the weather; while in the gymnasium he wore a frilled garment reaching a little above the knees. Besides this information, the *Manasollasa* mentions the different kinds of textile material used in designing the garment[69]

There are also references in the *Manasollasa* of the costumes of the ladies of the harem. They are said to have worn garments made of brocade, linen and cotton and tunics reaching the feet[70].

The officers dress comprised of an upper garment with long arms and comfortable turbans[71].

At another place, the articles of male costumes are concentrated. They comprise of a waist-cloth, a dupatta, narrow waist-bands, jackets, turbans and trousers of various kinds[72]. The warriors, bards, jesters etc., are said to have worn patterned stuffs and brocaded turban. Horsemen are said to have worn silk turbans and high tunics. At another place, the horsemen are said to have worn dupattas and jackets. The hunters are said to have worn green jackets, green turbans and trousers[73].

There are also references in the *Manasollasa* which throw light on the female costumes in the Deccan. The attendants wore their upper garment tied firmly. In general, the women from Andhra are said to have worn their upper garments on the right[74]. Thus a considerable amount of change has occurred since the 3rd or 4th century A.D. in the field of textiles and costumes, with the advent of Brahmanical form of art in 'Andhradesa'. Though the style of dressing in the upper classes remained the same with a few changes here and there. But there seems to be a slight progress in the mode of dressing as far as the commoners are concerned. The new developments noticed are the introduction of the dupatta, the jackets, trousers and most important is the introduction of a bodice in the female costumes, though it was not in vogue.

From the literary evidence of the Chalukyan period, much information was gathered regarding the material of the textile used, the colours, the prints and patterns etc. Besides, we get information of the Chief Centres of Manufacturing the textiles and the places of imports[75].

Constant warfare between the Chalukyas of Kalyana and the Cholas for the possession of the Chalukyan kingdom of Vengi weakened both the powers and in the latter half of the twelfth century, the Hoysalas of Dorasamudra, the Yadavas of Devagiri and Kakatiyas of Warangal became independent[76].

The evidence for the history of textiles and costumes in the period ranging from A.D. 700 to 1200 is almost wholly literary, as the sculptures of the period treat the costumes stylistically[77]. They show that essentially there was little difference between the Southern costumes and textiles and those of the other regions of India. The *Yasastilakacampu* of Somadeva composed in A.D. 959 during the reign of Rashtrakuta Krsna III (939-966) gives a better picture of the contemporary fabrics and costumes of the Deccan and other parts of India. The contemporary author Puspadanta also adds to, the meagre details of Deccan costume. Another contemporary source, the *Manasollasa*, (mentioned earlier) of the Western Chalukyan King, Somesvara gives details of costumes and textiles which were not only common in Karnataka but almost all over India[78].

The *Yasastilakacampu* gives a vivid picture of costumes worn by soldiers from different parts of the country assembled for military parade. The soldiers from the Deccan had their tangled top-knots tied with cloth-bands around their foreheads[79].

The *Yasastilakacampu* also gives some interesting details of the tenth century textile, *dukula*, a bark fibre of birch and kuja. At another place in the same source, a mixed linen silk stuff, known as *pattadukula*, is mentioned. Besides a list of some more interesting details of the contemporary fabrics is mentioned[80].

In general, it seems that in the twelfth century, jackets, tunics and trousers had become common articles of wear for the male and the female now became accustomed to wear a bodice to cover the breasts and the sari at this stage reached the ankles as is worn in the present day manner. Though the new trend in the style of wearing costumes is attested in earlier literature, it is possible that their common use shows greater contact with the outside world, especially, the Arabs and Persians. However, a Rashtrakuta painting of 9th century from Ellora[81] presents the following details:

The women in the painting are seen wearing a diaphanous, designed undergarment reaching a little below the knee. The undergarment is securely held at the waist by a *kamarbandh* which is decorated by beaded tassels. The hair is also covered by a scarf, the ends hanging by the side. The body above the waist is bare as usual.

The dress of the male also consists of a short lower garment secured by a *kamarbandh* with tassels hanging in the centre[82]. (Flying Vidyadharas, Ellora, Plate III, p.63)

In the simpler forms of primitive costumes, natural materials alone are used for, the most part flowers and leaves. At a higher level of sartorial development, more permanent artificial garments may be prepared from bark, cotton, flax or leather. The transition from primitive to tropical costume comes about through the increase in size of the garments originally suspend from the hip ring. The loin cloth or apron then becomes a skirt, which is indeed the characteristic and essential garment of tropical costume. The tropical costume mostly made from vegetable rather than from animal products and is associated with the further development of the art of weaving[83]. From the point of view, the depiction of costumes in the Nolamba Sculptures are interesting and varied.

During the Nolamba period, it is difficult to see any difference between the aristocratic persons and the commoners, either in articles of dress or in the way of wearing them. If at all there existed any difference it could have been obviously in the material. It is quite possible that the higher class of people must have used fine fabric while the commoners used simpler variety. As regards scantiness of the dress in the reliefs perhaps the persons depicted in the Nolamba sculptures were wearing a diaphanous costume scarcely visible to the naked eye[84].

It has been said that "Indian gods live like glorified rajas"[85]. The *gods and celestial beings* and the kings depicted in the sculptures wear a few items of dress. It includes an *antariya* and rarely *uttariya*. But a different type of lower garment occurs in the case of *Natesa*. He is shown wearing a cut-drawer resembling modern *janghia*. (Fig.II, 6, Pl.III)[86]. A deviation in the mode of wearing the lower garment can be seen in the case of god *Vishnu*. He is shown wearing a dhoti which extends upto his ankles. The dhoti is secured by a waist-band, the tassels of which slings gracefully in the centre, its loop set on the right side. (Fig.II, 7)[87]. The gods like Isana, Agni, Vayu, Varuna, Yama etc., appear with *ardhoruka*, indicating its popularity among one section of the aristocratic society. (Pl.IV)[88].

The *Vinadhara* offers a different type of dress. He is shown wearing a *langoti*. Over it round the waist is tied a strip of cloth, while the upper portion is left bare. (Fig.I, 2, pl.II)[89].

In one of the panels, the wrestlers dress is depicted. A panel depicts wrestling scene between Vali and Sugriva. Here the dress of Vali and Sugriva includes an *ardhoruka* tightly secured by a waist-band[90].

A panel depicts the scene of *amorous couples.* The males in the panel are seen wearing an *ardhoruka* secured by an elaborate waist-band. There is no upper garment. (Pl. XVIII)[91].

The Nolamba sculptures reveal scanty dress for the Goddesses. We find the same dress used by both the aristocratic persons and commonality. The goddess Uma[92], in a panel, is seen wearing an undergarment which reaches upto the ankles. It is seen secured by a girdle. The folds of the sari in sculptures is shown in clear lines. Her upper portion is left bare.

The goddess Kali[93], offers a different type of dress. She is shown wearing garment resembling the modern *janghia* and a breast band. This is the only example in the entire range of sculptures where the upper garment is shown as worn by a female.

In one of the panels, Parvati is seen wearing a Sari, secured by a *kamarbandh* which is further secured by a girdle. (Fig. III, 13, Pl.I)[94].

The sari worn by Ganga ends just over the knees. The panel shows the lower garment of Ganga is secured by a waist-band one end of which dangles on her left side. There is no upper garment. (Fig. III, Pl.X)[95].

The following are a few examples to show printed or designed saris that were in vogue during the Nolamba period[96]. On a slab, the wife of Vayu is shown wearing a printed or designed sari as her lower garment. The design or print over the sari is clearly sculptured. The sari ends over the thigh and the tassels of the waist-band tied round the sari for securing it, is clearly shown.

We see a different attire in the case of a celestial depicted on a jali window of a temple belonging to the Nolamba period. She is shown wearing a sari, which is having a print or design of a creeper alternated by hands. The sari ends below the knees and secured by a thick waist-band (Fig.V, 24)[97].

In the pair of human figures (amorous couples), the female wears only a lower garment. The sari extends upto the ankles. There is a waist-band securing the sari. There is no upper garment. The female dress in the amorous couples very much resembles that which is seen on the goddesses. They are represented almost bare-bodied, except for the use of a lower garment at times tied with a waist-band[98].

This panel depicts the costumes of soldiers[99]. A panel carved on the adhishtana of a temple, depicts a battle scene in the Ramayana. The soldiers are seen wearing a *ardhoruka* which is generally secured by a waist-band. In this particular panel, the soldier wears a short dhoti which ends over the thighs. The tassels of the dhoti slinging in the centre can be clearly seen. (Fig. VI, 29).

This is also a scene from the Ramayana. Here, the dress of the sages[100] is depicted. In this, the sages are shown wearing a dhoti which reaches upto the ankles. The dhoti is secured by a waist-band which at times consists of multicoils. No *uttariya* is seen on the upper body. The dress of the sages resemble very much the dress of the present days' saints. (Fig. VIII, 44).

From among the *commoners,* an idea about the attire of the *ganikas*[101] can be had from the sculpture depicted on the jali window of a temple of the Nolamba period. Here, he is shown wearing a langoti. (Fig. VI, 30).

A *male dancer*[102] is depicted on a Hero stone. Here he is shown wearing a short dhoti, which is secured by a waist-band. The tuft of the waist-band is seen slinging between the legs of the dancer. (Plate XIX).

A *female dancer*[103] is seen wearing a sari tucking one end of it at the back. The sari ends over the ankles and is tied tightly around the body, facilitating the easy dance for the dancer. She wears no *sthanottariya*. (Fig. VI, 32).

At another place on a jali window of a temple, a female dancer is shown wearing only a lower garment. It appears to be a single piece of long apparel which is tied around the loins. The lower garment extends upto the ankles. (Fig. VIII, 33)[104].

In a relief on the window of a temple[105], two dancers reveal an interesting mode of wearing a sari. They wear a lower garment in an interesting manner. The sari worn by them completely covers the right leg while the left leg is left bare. The tufts of the sari sling in the centre and on the left thigh of the dancers. The folds of the sari are clearly seen. The dress very much resembles that of the present day dancers. (Fig. VII, 35 and 36).

On a Hero Stone[106], a female dancer is seen wearing a sari which ends over the thighs. It is secured by a waist-band. The sari is worn tightly around the loins and the folds are clearly sculptured. (Fig. VII, 37).

The figures of *Musicians*[107] are seen sculpted in different temples of the Nolamba period. From these, we can get a glimpse of the costumes and dress worn by the musicians. On a perforated window of a temple, a female Vina player is shown wearing a sari as her lower garment. The sari is seen wrapped round the loins and reaches the knees. The border of the sari is clearly seen. (Fig. VIII, 41).

In another temple, a female flutist[108] seen in different attire. She is shown wearing a sari which ends at the knees. The garment is secured by a waist-band. The folds of the sari are clearly visible. There is no upper garment. (Fig. VIII, 42).

Another scene on the *adhishtana* of the same temple mentioned above can be seen, a cymbal player[109] who offers yet another dress. Here, the sari is wound around the waist in multi-coils, giving an appearance of a schematic rib-like design while the one end of the sari slings in between the legs in tassels. As usual, no upper garment is used. (Fig. VIII, 43).

The introduction of tunics, trousers, jackets etc., into the arena of field of costumes had now gained popularity in the Nolamba period. In the preceding centuries it was observed that, new styles were evolved in wearing the already exsiting garments like saris, dhotis etc. But the Nolambas practised these new styles in their daily life. For example - a soldier wore the dhoti according to his convenience and a dancer wore the sari according to her convenience during swift movements of the dance. If these were the main changes, some sections of the people remain unchanged in their mode of attire. The dress of the aristocratic section, still, went on with the old fashion. Their dress very much resembles that seen on the Gods and Goddesses.

The sculptures of the Kakatiya dynasty show *male* figures wearing a dhoti in different styles.

The male dress generally consisted of a turban, an upper garment and a dhoti which covered the loins. Sometimes the dhoti is worn tightly and it clings to the legs. The sculptures of *soldiers* generally reveal this fashion. It helps them in their swift movements. The *ascetics* are seen wearing a *kaupina* or a small piece of cloth in the middle[110].

The dress of the female images during the Kakatiya times generally consist of a lower garment, such as a sari and upper garment includes scarf or bodice. *Cholika* was one of the most important garments of women and they used to put it on for covering their chest region. The breast garment called *kanchuki* covers the breasts only. The sari was the most important and popular item of dress for women. It was almost as it is worn in modern times. The sculputres reveal that *ladies from the upper class* of society always wore the sari reaching down to their feet. The sari of the *poorer sections* of the community reached either upto the knees or slightly below the knees. The sari was usually fastened round the waist, a part of it was converted into graceful pleats and tucked in front and the other end dangling downwards and finally thrown over the shoulders to wrap the upper part of the body[111].

Most of the female figures during the Kakatiya period both divine and human are shown without an upper garment. The portion above the waist is often seen undraped. Modern scholars have different opinions about the bareness of the upper part of the women and they differ in their conclusions. Cunningham thought that nudity conveyed no sense of indecency in India prior to the advent of the Muslims. So women in sculptures dressed. Charles Fabri states that in the whole of history of Indian art from the earliest to approximately the 12th century A.D. women are invariably shown as wearing no garment to cover their breasts. It appears that women of all classes went about bare from the waist upwards for many hundreds of years[112].

Before examining the sculputres of the Vijayanagara period, an account of some foreign travellers who visited the kingdom and left valuable records of their observations would be interesting at this jucture. A realistic picture of the costumes of Krishnadeva Raya and his women was given by Domingo Paes[113]. According to him, the king was clothed in certain white clothes embroidered with many roses in gold and wore diamonds in his neck. On his head, the king, had a cap of brocade, in fashion like a Galacian helmet, covered with a piece of fine stuff of fine silk and he was bare-footed. As a custom in the contemporary period, the king is said to have presented Paes, a cloth embroidered with many pretty figures. This was a token of friendship and love.

According to Varthema[114], a Portuguese traveller, the costumes of the people of Vijayanagara are as follows: "The men of condition wear a short skirt, and on their head a cloth of gold and silk but nothing on the feet. The common people go quite naked with the exception of a piece of cloth about the middle. The king wears a cap of gold broacade two spans long, and when he goes to war he wears a quilted dress of cotton, and over it he puts another garment full of golden piasters."

According to Barbosa[115] "The women go trimly clad, their men wear certain clothes as a girdle below, wound very tightly in many folds and white shirts of cotton or silk or coarse brocade which are gathered between thighs but open in front: on their heads they carry small turbans and some wear silk or brocade caps. They also wear other large garments thrown over their shoulders like caps."

Costumes and Dress as Gleaned through the Sculptures of the Vijayanagara period

On the South gopura of a temple[116] of the Vijayanagara period is a figure of a *King*. The figure is shown standing erect with hands in *anjali mudra*. He wears a tall conical cap in the typical Vijayanagara style. He wears an undergarment extending upto the ankles. The tassels of the waist-band are seen in the centre. (Pl.LX1-1).

At another place, the king is seen wearing a tall conical cap and an undergarment upto the knees. Here, the folds of the garment are prominent. Here, the queen is seen wearing an undergarment reaching a little above the ankles. The undergarment is secured by a *kamarbandh* with a long pleated tassel touching the ground. The folds of the pleated undergarment are significant[117].

The paintings on the ceilings and murals found extant in the temples of the Vijayanagara period also serve as an excellent source for studying the textiles and costumes; the dress and garments in vogue during the period and also the prevailing fashions of garments besides the colour and texture of the material, the prints and designs etc. In the following painted panels we get a glimpse of the contemporary dress, the colours, the material etc., worn by different sections of the people.

A scene depicting Rama's Marriage[118]. In this painting we get a glimpse of the costumes worn by the Royal people. Here the male are seen wearing an undergarment secured at the waist by a *kamarbandh*.

The female figures are seen wearing the lower garment in the present day's style of wearing a sari along with a blouse covering the upper part of the body.

In another scene[119] Vidyaranya taken in procession, we get a glimpse of the costumes worn by different people of the contemporary society. Such as :

1. Noble Class
2. The Palanquin bearers
3. Trumpeteers
4. The Mahout
5. Banner-bearers
6. Chamara-bearers (Plate V)

A 16th century painted panel in the Lepakshi temple depicts for the first time, foreign impact in the field of costume. The male figures in this picture are seen wearing an upper garment, a lower garment and an elongated cap. The upper garment consists of a shirt, sewn in the fashion of the present days' 'Kurta' with long sleeves (S.No.51, M.No.68-XXIV-A Kurta from Benaras). The undergarment is a dhoti, secured by a designed *kamarbandh* with central tassels. The elongated caps resemble the Persian Caps which are also designed.

There is another interesting painted panel in the Lepakshi Temple[120] which also belongs to the 16th century. This panel is interesting for it depicts a caparisoned cow. In the same panel can be seen Siva, Parvati, King, Queen, Royal attendants etc. The details of the costumes worn by each character in the painting is as follows:

Siva, can be seen seated on a caparisoned cow. He is seen wearing an undergarment. It is noticed that the garment is the skin of a tiger.

Parvati, is seen seated behind Siva on the same cow. She is seen wearing an undergarment reaching upto the ankles. The garment has some design on it. There is no upper garment.

The next character in the painting is the *King*. He is seen wearing a designed undergarment secured by a waist-band which is also designed. A designed upper garment a *uttariya* is seen passing below the arms.

The *Queen* in the painting is seen wearing a bordered undergarment extending a little below the knees. There is no upper garment.

One more character is a *royal attendant*. The dress of the women is interesting for she is seen covering her bosom with a designed cloth. She is seen wearing an undergarment reaching the knees and secured by a waist-band.

A painting of the Cuddapah School[121], 17th century, depicts different people in different costumes. The painting is divided into several sections. In one of the sections Yama is shown seated on a wooden couch with his back resting against a cushion. For the first time, we notice a designed floor carpet. Besides the costumes of the people, we can also notice the caparisoned animals - an elephant, a horse and a cow.

The Sultanate Period

The material for this period can be gathered from literary sources.

In general, the Kings wore tight fitting trousers, a tight-sleeved long coat fitting up to the waist. The Kings wore a closely tied turban. The dress of the royal women resembled that of Persian princesses.

The Hindu women during this period covered their bosom. *Choli,* a tight-fitting and half-sleeved dress was evolved. It was quite different from the persian garment. It covered only the front portion in the initial stage of its evolution. The two side edges of the *choli* were tied with strings at the back which remained, as ever, bare. With the passage of time the *choli* gathered a full circle to cover the back.

References

1. Krishna Sastry, V.V. (ed.) *The Andhra Pradesh Journal of Archaeology,* Vol.I, 1979, pp.89-90.
2. Ibid, p.90.
3. Ibid, p.181.
4. Ibid,
5. Ibid,
6. Ibid, p.93.
7. Ibid, p.95.
8. Nigam, M.L. *Sculptural Heritage of Andhradesa,* 1980, p.26.
9. Ibid, p.26.
10. Ibid.

11. Moti Chandra, *Costumes, Textiles, Cosmetics and Coiffure,* Delhi, 1973, p.20.
12. Ibid.
13. Ibid.
14. Ibid.
15. Ibid, p.21.
16. Ibid.
17. Ibid.
18. Ibid.
19. Ibid.
20. Margabandhu, C. *Archaeology of the Satavahana-Kshatrapa Times,* Delhi, 1985, p.172.
21. Ibid, p.205.
22. Ibid, p.206.
23. Ibid, p.234.
24. Moti Chandra, *Op.Cit.,* 1973, p.25.
25. Rajendraprasad, B. *Art of South India - Andhra Pradesh,* Delhi,1980, p.40.
26. Ibid, p.42.
27. Ibid, p.43.
28. Rajendraprasad, B. *Op.Cit.*, 1980, p.44.
29. Ibid.
30. Krishna Murthy, K. *Nagarjunakonda - A Cultural Study,* 1977, Delhi, p.36.
31. Ibid, p.37 & 38.
32. Ibid, p.38.
33. Ibid, p.39.
34. Ibid, p.42.
35. Ibid.
36. Ibid, p.39.
37. Ramachandra, T.N. *Bulletin Madras Government Museum* Vol. I, Part-I, p.16.
38. Krishna Murthy, K. *Op.Cit.*, 1977, p.43.
39. Ibid, p.44.
40. Ibid, p.39.
41. Ibid, p.43.
42. Ibid, p.40.
43. Ibid.
44. Ibid, p.40.
45. Ibid, p.41.
46. Ibid.
47. Ibid, p.50.
48. Ibid, p.51.
49. Ibid.
50. Ibid, p.52.
51. Ibid, p.45.
52. Ibid, p.46.
53. Ibid, p.50.
54. Ibid, p.55.
55. Moti Chandra, *Op.Cit.*, 1973, p.42.
56. Ramachandra, T.N. *Op.Cit.*, 1977, p.9.

57. Krishna Murthy, K. *Op.Cit.*, 1977, p.53.
58. Ibid.
59. Ibid.
60. Ibid, p.54.
61. Ramachandra, T.N. *Op.Cit.*, 1980, pp.6, 7.
62. Rajendra Prasad, B. *Op.Cit.*, 1980, p.59.
63. Ibid, p.70.
64. Rajendra Prasad, B. *Chalukyan Temples of Andhra Pradesh,* New Delhi, 1983, p.80.
65. Ibid, p.80.
66. Ibid, p.81.
67. Ibid, p.96.
68. Moti Chandra, *Op.Cit.*, 1973, p.122.
69. Ibid, p.122.
70. Ibid, p.123.
71. Ibid, p.122.
72. Ibid, p.123.
73. Ibid, p.122.
74. Ibid, p.123.
75. Ibid, pp.123-124.
76. Ibid, p.104.
77. Ibid.
78. Ibid, p.120.
79. Ibid.
80. Ibid, p.121.
81. Sivarama Murthi, C. *The Vijaynagar Paintings,* 1985, p.17.
82. Krishna Murthy, K. *Nolamba Sculptures - A Cultural Study,* New Delhi, 1987, p.10.
83. Ibid, p.11.
84. Ibid, p.11.
85. Ibid.
86. Ibid, p.12.
87. Ibid.
88. Ibid.
89. Ibid.
90. Ibid, p.13.
91. Ibid.
92. Ibid, p.14.
93. Ibid, p.14.
94. Ibid.
95. Ibid, p.15.
96. Ibid.
97. Ibid, p.16.
98. Ibid.
99. Ibid.
100. Ibid, p.20.
101. Ibid, p.18.
102. Ibid, p.19.

103. Ibid.
104. Ibid.
105. Ibid.
106. Ibid.
107. Ibid, p.20
108. Ibid.
109. Ibid.
110. Ramanaiah, J. *Temples of South India,* New Delhi, 1989, p.215.
111. Ibid, p.214.
112. Ibid, p.214.
113. Moti Chandra, *Op.Cit.,* 1973, p.177.
114. Ibid.
115. Ibid.
116. Kameswara Rao, V. *Select Vijaynagar Temples of Rayalaseema,* Hyderabad, 1976, p.141.
117. Ibid, p.192.
118. Sivarama Murthi, C. *Op.Cit.,* p.65.
119. Ibid.
120. Sivarama Murthi, C. *Op.Cit.,* 1985, p.69.
121. Ibid, p.70.

CHAPTER - II

DESCRIPTIVE CATALOGUE OF TEXTILES

I. SALAR JUNG MUSEUM, HYDERABAD

The total number of textiles on display in the Salar Jung Museum, Hyderabad is one hundred and twenty. Of these 107 are exhibited in Room No.6 of the Museum and is named as the "Indian Textile" Gallery. The rest of them i.e., 13 pieces of the total textiles included in this study are displayed in Room No.3 which is named "Bronze and Painted Textiles" Gallery. The textiles are classified into the following materials (A) Cotton (B) Silk (C) Woollen and (D) Mixed Fabrics.

The total number of textiles under each material is :

(A)	Cotton	-	38
(B)	Silk	-	16
(C)	Woollen	-	10
(D)	Mixed	-	50
(E)	Others	-	06

Among these there are some sewn garments which comprise of Chogas, Sherwanis, Chowbagla (which is also a kind of upper garment); Bridal dress, Kurtas, Angarkhas etc. The other textiles on display include Kimkhobs, Himrus, Shawls, Saris, Odhnis, Dupattas, Turbans, Kamarbandhs, Patkas and Furnishing materials like Curtains, Sheets, Bed Covers, Cushion Covers, Palanquin Covers, Tray Covers, Cloth Pieces etc.

The textiles on exhibition belong to different periods. The earliest piece belongs to the 16th century A.D. and the latest textile displayed belongs to the 20th century. A period-wise classification is as follows :

16th century Textiles	-	Serial Nos. 12, 19
17th century Textiles	-	Serial No. 1
Late 17th century Textiles	-	Serial No. 98
18th century Textiles	-	Serial Nos. 3, 5, 20, 48, 79, 96, 107, 108, 118
Early 18th century Textiles	-	Serial Nos. 112
Late 18th century Textiles	-	Serial Nos. 14, 17
19th century Textiles	-	Serial Nos. 2, 4, 6 to 11, 13, 16, 18, 23 to 26, 28, to 30, 32 to 34, 37 to 39, 42 to 44 49 to 56, 58 to 67, 71, 73 to 75, 77, 78, 80 to 83, 86 to 94, 97, 101, 102, 104, 105, 109 to 111, 113, 117, 119
Early 19th century Textiles	-	Serial Nos. 22, 70, 72, 85, 95, 120

Mid 19th century Textiles	-	Serial Nos. 27, 106
Late 19th century Textiles	-	Serial Nos. 40, 46, 68, 69, 84, 103, 114, 115
20th century Textiles	-	Serial Nos. 15, 21, 31, 35, 36, 41, 57, 99, 100
Early 20th century Textiles	-	Serial Nos. 45, 76

The period for Serial No.47 is not mentioned and the date for textile with Serial No.116 is assigned to 1840 A.D.

The textiles exhibited belong to different regions across the country, from Kashmir to Kancheepuram and from Gujarat to Dacca. They include the famous fabrics of the different regions like the Kashmir Shawls, Phulkaris of Punjab, Patolas of Gujarat, Brocades of Benaras, Muslins of Dacca, Painted Pichchwais of Rajasthan, Himrus and Kinkhobs of Deccan, Saris from Chanderi, Venkatagiri and Kancheepuram and Kalamkaris from Palakollu, Kalahasti and Machilipatnam etc. The various textile objects are displayed in thirteen different show-cases. A detailed study of each object is made in the following manner :

Serial No.	-	1
Show-case No. & M.No.	-	(1) - (62-11)
Fabric	-	Mixed
Specific Type	-	Choga
School/Place	-	Deccan
Period	-	17th century
Description	-	The choga or tunic is maroon in colour. It consists of tree design in vertical panels. It is a mixed fabric woven in cotton and silk threads.

Serial No.	-	2 (Plate 1)
Show-case No. & M.No.	-	(1) - (94/XXV)
Fabric	-	Mixed (Brocade)
Specific Type	-	Kimkhob
School/Place	-	Deccan
Period	-	19th century
Description	-	This mixed fabric consists of a zari body depicting flower designs in gold.

Serial No.	-	3
Show-case No. & M.No.	-	(1) - (62-31-1)
Fabric	-	Mixed
Specific Type	-	Choga
School/Place	-	Deccan
Period	-	18th century
Description	-	The choga is made of mixed cotton and silk fibres. The background colour is yellow with purple and red floral designs in panels.

Serial No.	-	4
Show-case No. & M.No.	-	(1) - (6/XXV)

Fabric	-	Mixed
Specific Type	-	Himroo
School/Place	-	Deccan
Period	-	19th century
Description	-	The body colour of this mixed fabric is grey. It is woven in gold zari. The design woven is the leaf pattern.
Serial No.	-	5 (Plate 2)
Show-case No. & M.No.	-	(1) - (62-84)
Fabric	-	Mixed
Specific Type	-	Sherwani
School/Place	-	Deccan
Period	-	18th century
Description	-	The body colour of this sherwani is yellow and is embroidered with flower plant pattern.
Serial No.	-	6
Show-case No. & M.No.	-	(1) - (108/XXV)
Fabric	-	Mixed
Specific Type	-	Kimkhob
School/Place	-	India
Period	-	19th century
Description	-	The body colour of this mixed fabric is maroon. The fabric is woven with gold thread in panels consisting of flower patterns.
Serial No.	-	7 (Plate 3)
Show-case No. & M.No.	-	(1) - (84/XXIV)
Fabric	-	Mixed (Brocade)
Specific Type	-	Chowbagla
School/Place	-	Western India
Period	-	19th century
Description	-	The chowbagla on display is in pink colour and is brocaded in zari.
Serial No.	-	8
Show-case No. & M.No.	-	(1) - (21/XL)
Fabric	-	Cotton
Specific Type	-	Cloth
School/Place	-	Punjab
Period	-	19th century
Description	-	This cotton cloth from Punjab is black in colour. It is embroidered in phulkari work.
Serial No.	-	9
Show-case No. & M.No.	-	(1) - (87-XLII)

Fabric - Velvet
Specific Type - Cloth Piece
School/Place - India
Period - 19th century
Description - The cloth piece is yellow in colour embroidered with a pattern of tree with yellow flowers and green leaves.

Serial No. - 10
Show-case No. & M.No. - (1) - (4-XXVII)
Fabric - Cotton
Specific Type - Sheet
School/Place - India
Period - 19th century
Description - This is a printed sheet. The design resembles the Kalamkari prints of South India.

Serial No. - 11
Show-case No. & M.No. - (2) - (55/XXV)
Fabric - Woollen
Specific Type - Shawl
School/Place - Kashmir
Period - 19th century
Description - This shawl from Kashmir is made up of black and green background. It consists of a circular panel with a vase design in the centre.

Serial No. - 12
Show-case No. & M.No. - (2) - (50/XXV)
Fabric - Woollen
Specific Type - Shawl
School/Place - Kashmir
Period - 16th century
Description - This is a red woollen shawl from Kashmir. It is decorated with embroidery of yellow floral patterns.

Serial No. - 13
Show-case No. & M.No. - (2) - (62-15)
Fabric - Woollen
Specific Type - Shawl
School/Place - Kashmir
Period - 19th century
Description - This is a black Kashmir shawl embroidered with floral designs.

Serial No. - 14
Show-case No. & M.No. - (2) - (424-XLIV)

Fabric - Woollen
Specific Type - Shawl
School/Place - Kashmir
Period - Late 18th century
Description - This is a red Kashmir shawl. The fabric is woollen. It is decorated with yellow and black floral designs in embroidery.

Serial No. - 15
Show-case No. & M.No. - (2) - (53/XLII)
Fabric - Mixed
Specific Type - Bed Sheet
School/Place - India
Period - 20th century
Description - This Bed-sheet is made of silk, woollen and cotton fibres. The body colour is brown.

Serial No. - 16
Show-case No. & M.No. - (2) - (64-47)
Fabric - Cotton
Specific Type - Bed Sheet
School/Place - India
Period - 19th century
Description - This cotton sheet with white background consists of beautifully embroidered flowers all over.

Serial No. - 17
Show-case No. & M.No. - (2) - (46/XXV)
Fabric - Woollen
Specific Type - Shawl
School/Place - Kashmir
Period - Late 18th century
Description - This red Woollen shawl from Kashmir consists of flower plant designs in embroidery.

Serial No. - 18
Show-case No. & M.No. - (2) - (48-XXV)
Fabric - Mixed Fabric
Specific Type - Shawl
School/Place - India
Period - 19th century
Description - The white shawl is woven with turanj shape panels and floral designs all over.

Serial No. - 19
Show-case No. & M.No. - (2) - (40/XXV)

Fabric	-	Woollen
Specific Type	-	Shawl
School/Place	-	India
Period	-	16th century
Description	-	The body colour of the shawl is mixed white and yellow. It is decorated with floral designs of different colours.
Serial No.	-	20
Show-case No. & M.No.	-	(2) - (43-XXV)
Fabric	-	Woollen
Specific Type	-	Shawl
School/Place	-	Kashmir
Period	-	18th century
Description	-	The base of this shawl is made of white wool. It consists of floral designs embroidered all over.
Serial No.	-	21
Show-case No. & M.No.	-	(2) - (21-XXXIII)
Fabric	-	Cotton
Specific Type	-	Curtain
School/Place	-	India
Period	-	20th century
Description	-	This curtain made of cotton is having a printed pattern consisting of stalks and leaves in green with blue and red flowers.
Serial No.	-	22
Show-case No. & M.No.	-	(2) - (51-XXV)
Fabric		Woollen
Specific Type	-	Shawl
School/Place	-	Kashmir
Period	-	Early 19th century
Description	-	This green woollen shawl consists of beautifully embroidered flower patterns.
Serial No.	-	23
Show-case No. & M.No.	-	(3) - (62-18)
Fabric	-	Cotton
Specific Type	-	Sari
School/Place	-	Udaipur (Rajasthan)
Period	-	19th century
Description	-	The material of this cotton sari is coarse and is locally called as Chhapala Sari. It is in majenta colour consisting of tinsel print. The design is flower with stalk and leaves.

Serial No.	-	24
Show-case No. & M.No.	-	(3) - (62-38-1)
Fabric	-	Cotton
Specific Type	-	Sari
School/Place	-	Gujarat
Period	-	19th century
Description	-	This cotton sari from Gujarat is red in colour consisting of embroidery work in flower pattern.

Serial No.	-	25
Show-case No. & M.No.	-	(3) - (67-XXV)
Fabric	-	Silk (Brocade)
Specific Type	-	Sari
School/Place	-	Benaras
Period	-	19th century
Description	-	This is a beautiful brocade saree from Benaras. The body colour is light green with a majenta coloured border. The entire sari is woven with silver zari in panels.

Serial No.	-	26
Show-case No. & M.No.	-	(4) - (77-XXV)
Fabric	-	Silk
Specific Type	-	Sari
School/Place	-	Kancheepuram-South India
Period	-	19th century
Description	-	This black silk sari from Kancheepuram is woven all over with zari checks and a zari border. The pallou and the border is woven in red colour.

Serial No.	-	27
Show-case No. & M.No.	-	(4) - (154-XXV)
Fabric	-	Cotton
Specific Type	-	Bed Cover
School/Place	-	Kalamkari-Machilipatnam
Period	-	Mid 19th century
Description	-	This maroon coloured bed spread from Machilipatnam is painted with Kalamkari work. The design consists of small leaf pattern on blue ground all over.

Serial No.	-	28 (Plate 4)
Show-case No. & M.No.	-	(5) - (79-XXV)
Fabric	-	Cotton
Specific Type	-	Sari
School/Place	-	Venkatagiri, Andhra Pradesh

Period	-	19th century
Description	-	This is a red cotton sari from Venkatagiri in Andhra Pradesh. It consists of zari lines making square patterns.

Serial No.	-	29
Show-case No. & M.No.	-	(5) - (76-XXV)
Fabric	-	Silk
Specific Type	-	Sari
School/Place	-	Chanderi
Period	-	19th century
Description	-	On display in this showcase is a red Chanderi Sari. Chanderi is situated a few miles from Gwalior and is the original home of Chanderi fabrics. The sari consists of a zari flower border.

Serial No.	-	30
Show-case No. & M.No.	-	(5) - (64-XXV)
Fabric	-	Silk (Brocade)
Specific Type	-	Sari
School/Place	-	Benaras
Period	-	19th century
Description	-	This is a light mauve coloured brocaded sari with a navy blue border.

Serial No.	-	31
Show-case No. & M.No.	-	(5) - (80-41)
Fabric	-	Silk (Brocade)
Specific Type	-	Sari
School/Place	-	Benaras
Period	-	20th century
Description	-	This is a green coloured sari from Benaras. It is also a brocaded sari with gold zari making a check pattern.

Serial No.	-	32
Show-case No. & M.No.	-	(5) - (59-XXV)
Fabric	-	Mixed (Brocade)
Specific Type	-	Odhni
School/Place	-	Benaras
Period	-	19th century
Description	-	This odhni from Benaras is woven with silk and cotton fibres. It is a mixed fabric consisting of different colours in each quarter.

Serial No.	-	33
Show-case No. & M.No.	-	(5) - (30-XXV)
Fabric	-	Mixed (Brocade)

Specific Type	-	Dupatta
School/Place	-	Benaras
Period	-	19th century
Description	-	This Dupatta from Benaras is also a mixed fabric in red colour. It consists of a flower pattern in zari.

Serial No.	-	34
Show-case No. & M.No.	-	(5) - (191-XXV)
Fabric	-	Mixed (Brocade)
Specific Type	-	Dupatta
School/Place	-	Benaras
Period	-	19th century
Description	-	This Dupatta from Benaras is also a mixed fabric in red colour. It consists of a flower pattern in zari.

Serial No.	-	35 (Plate 5)
Show-case No. & M.No.	-	(5) - (80-42)
Fabric	-	Mixed (Brocade)
Specific Type	-	Sari
School/Place	-	Benaras
Period	-	20th century
Description	-	This richly brocaded zari sari consists of a heavy zari pallou with Turanj pattern in the corner.

Serial No.	-	36 (Plate 6)
Show-case No. & M.No.	-	(5) - (80-40)
Fabric	-	Mixed (Brocade)
Specific Type	-	Sari
School/Place	-	Benaras
Period	-	20th century
Description	-	This is a zari brocade sari with a red centre. There are diamond designs all over.

Serial No.	-	37
Show-case No. & M.No.	-	(5) - (192-XXV)
Fabric	-	Mixed (Brocade)
Specific Type	-	Dupatta
School/Place	-	Benaras
Period	-	19th century
Description	-	This is a red coloured dupatta with Silver zari floral pattern.

Serial No.	-	38
Show-case No. & M.No.	-	(5) - (88-XXV)
Fabric	-	Mixed (Brocade)

Specific Type - Odhni
School/Place - Benaras
Period - 19th century
Description - This is a dark red Odhni. This is also a brocade with zari in floral pattern.

Serial No. - 39
Show-case No. & M.No. - (5) - (105-XXV)
Fabric - Mixed (Brocade)
Specific Type - Dupatta
School/Place - Benaras
Period - 19th century
Description - This is a green coloured Benaras brocade having zari flowers.

Serial No. - 40 (Plate 7)
Show-case No. & M.No. - (6) - (62-26)
Fabric - Mixed
Specific Type - Choga
School/Place - Aurangabad
Period - Late 19th century
Description - This Choga consists of blue and white stripe.

Serial No. - 41
Show-case No. & M.No. - (6) - (65-XLII)
Fabric - Cotton
Specific Type - Curtain
School/Place - Punjab
Period - 20th century
Description - It is a black curtain embroidered with floral pattern in orange coloured thread.

Serial No. - 42
Show-case No. & M.No. - (6) - (1-XXII)
Fabric - Cotton
Specific Type - Curtain
School/Place - Punjab
Period - 19th century
Description - This is a dark brown phulkari curtain from Punjab embroidered with floral and turanj patterns.

Serial No. - 43
Show-case No. & M.No. - (6) - (22-XVI)
Fabric - Cotton
Specific Type - Cover

School/Place	-	Kashmir
Period	-	19th century
Description	-	This red coloured cover consists of embroidery work in green and black threads to make a compartmental design.
Serial No.	-	44
Show-case No. & M.No.	-	(6) - (65-XLII)
Fabric	-	Cotton
Specific Type	-	Curtain
School/Place	-	Punjab
Period	-	19th century
Description	-	This is an orange and brown curtain embroidered with Phulkari work. The Shishadar phulkari produced gives a striking effect.
Serial No.	-	45
Show-case No. & M.No.	-	(6) - (62-31-4)
Fabric	-	Mixed (Himroo)
Specific Type	-	Choga
School/Place	-	India
Period	-	Early 20th century
Description	-	This is a blue choga consisting of paisley pattern.
Serial No.	-	46
Show-case No. & M.No.	-	(7) - (78-XXIV)
Fabric	-	Mixed
Specific Type	-	Bride's Dress
School/Place	-	India
Period	-	Late 19th century
Description	-	The bride's dress on display is richly decorated with sequins, pearls etc. The embroidery work is done entirely in golden zari.
Serial No.	-	47
Show-case No. & M.No.	-	(7) - (40-XXIV)
Fabric	-	Woollen
Specific Type	-	Shawl
School/Place	-	Kashmir
Period	-	—
Description	-	The red coloured woollen shawl is embroidered with turanj designs.
Serial No.	-	48
Show-case No. & M.No.	-	(7) - (42-XXV)

Fabric	-	Woollen
Specific Type	-	Shawl
School/Place	-	India
Period	-	18th century
Description	-	This golden coloured woollen shawl is embroidered with different coloured threads in vertical panels.

Serial No.	-	49 (Plate 8)
Show-case No. & M.No.	-	(7) - (79-39)
Fabric	-	Silk
Specific Type	-	Curtain/Pichchwai
School/Place	-	India
Period	-	19th century
Description	-	This cream colour silk curtain is embroidered with shikarga scenes.

Serial No.	-	50 (Plate 9)
Show-case No. & M.No.	-	(7) - (79-40)
Fabric	-	Cotton
Specific Type	-	Pichchwai
School/Place	-	Deccan
Period	-	19th century
Description	-	The zari embroidered pichchwai depicts the scene of a shrine.

Serial No.	-	51 (Plate 10)
Show-case No. & M.No.	-	(7) - (68-XXIV)
Fabric	-	Mixed
Specific Type	-	Kurta
School/Place	-	Benaras
Period	-	19th century
Description	-	This kurta is pink in colour and consists of floral designs and karchobi borders on the neck.

Serial No.	-	52
Show-case No. & M.No.	-	(7) - (3-XXIV)
Fabric	-	Velvet
Specific Type	-	Palanquin Cover
School/Place	-	India
Period	-	19th century
Description	-	The Palanquin cover is embroidered with golden zari.

Serial No.	-	53
Show-case No. & M.No.	-	(7) - (25-XXV)

Fabric	-	Mixed
Specific Type	-	Turban
School/Place	-	India
Period	-	19th century
Description	-	The turban is completely woven with silver zari.

Serial No.	-	54
Show-case No. & M.No.	-	(7) - (2-XXIV)
Fabric	-	Velvet
Specific Type	-	Palanquin cover
School/Place	-	India
Period	-	19th century
Description	-	The palanquin cover consists of gold embroidered panels.

Serial No.	-	55
Show-case No. & M.No.	-	(7) - (6-XLIX)
Fabric	-	Velvet
Specific Type	-	Hand-Fan
School/Place	-	Lucknow
Period	-	19th century
Description	-	The hand fan is embroidered with karchobi pattern.

Serial No.	-	56
Show-case No. & M.No.	-	(7) - (367-XLIX)
Fabric	-	Velvet
Specific Type	-	Hand Fan
School/Place	-	Lucknow
Period	-	19th century
Description	-	The hand fan is embroidered with karchobi pattern.

Serial No.	-	57
Show-case No. & M.No.	-	(7) - (56-XXIV)
Fabric	-	Velvet
Specific Type	-	Cushion Cover
School/Place	-	India
Period	-	20th century
Description	-	The purple colour cushion cover for masnad is embroidered with zari work depicting flower patterns.

Serial No.	-	58
Show-case No. & M.No.	-	(8) - (104-XXIV)
Fabric	-	Mixed (Brocade)
Specific Type	-	Tash
School/Place	-	India

Period	-	19th century
Description	-	The mixed fabric is woven with silver zari depicting floral designs.
Serial No.	-	59
Show-case No. & M.No.	-	(8) - (98-XXIV)
Fabric	-	Mixed (Brocade)
Specific Type	-	Tash
School/Place	-	India
Period	-	19th century
Description	-	This fabric is woven in golden zari depicting floral stalk pattern.
Serial No.	-	60
Show-case No. & M.No.	-	(8) - (99-XXIV)
Fabric	-	Mixed (Brocade)
Specific Type	-	Tash
School/Place	-	India
Period	-	19th century
Description	-	This mixed fabric is woven with golden zari depicting flower pattern.
Serial No.	-	61
Show-case No. & M.No.	-	(8) - (96-XXIV)
Fabric	-	Mixed (Brocade)
Specific Type	-	Tash
School/Place	-	India
Period	-	19th century
Description	-	This silver tash consists of zari lozenge panels with red and green flowers.
Serial No.	-	62
Show-case No. & M.No.	-	(8) - (103-XXIV)
Fabric	-	Mixed (Brocade)
Specific Type	-	Tash
School/Place	-	India
Period	-	19th century
Description	-	This mixed fabric is woven with golden zari depicting flower pattern.
Serial No.	-	63
Show-case No. & M.No.	-	(8) - (97-XXIV)
Fabric	-	Mixed (Brocade)
Specific Type	-	Tash
School/Place	-	India

Period	-	19th century
Description	-	This mixed fabric is woven with golden zari depicting flower pattern.

Serial No.	-	64
Show-case No. & M.No.	-	(8) - (87-XXIV)
Fabric	-	Mixed
Specific Type	-	Kimkhob
School/Place	-	India
Period	-	19th century
Description	-	The red colour mixed fabric is woven with golden and silver flower pattern.

Serial No.	-	65
Show-case No. & M.No.	-	(8) - (160-XXV)
Fabric	-	Mixed
Specific Type	-	Cloth (Brocade)
School/Place	-	Benaras
Period	-	19th century
Description	-	This is a brocaded cloth.

Serial No.	-	66
Show-case No. & M.No.	-	(8) - (106-XXV)
Fabric	-	Mixed (Himroo)
Specific Type	-	Cloth
School/Place	-	Aurangabad
Period	-	19th century
Description	-	This is a brocaded cloth.

Serial No.	-	67
Show-case No. & M.No.	-	(8) - (141-XXV)
Fabric	-	Mixed
Specific Type	-	Cloth
School/Place	-	India
Period	-	19th century
Description	-	The cloth is pink in colour with OGEE Panels.

Serial No.	-	68
Show-case No. & M.No.	-	(8) - (172-XXV)
Fabric	-	Himroo
Specific Type	-	Cloth
School/Place	-	India
Period	-	Late 19th century
Description	-	This mixed fabric consists zari flower designs and is vermillion coloured.

Serial No.	-	69
Show-case No. & M.No.	-	(8) - (213-XXV)
Fabric	-	Mixed
Specific Type	-	Odhni
School/Place	-	Benaras
Period	-	Late 19th century
Description	-	This green colour odhni is depicted with silver flower-creeper design.

Serial No.	-	70
Show-case No. & M.No.	-	(8) - (174-XXV)
Fabric	-	Silk
Specific Type	-	Patka
School/Place	-	India
Period	-	Early 19th century
Description	-	This dark green silk patka is decorated with dotted designs.

Serial No.	-	71
Show-case No. & M.No.	-	(8) - (179-XXV)
Fabric	-	Silk
Specific Type	-	Patka
School/Place	-	Benaras
Period	-	19th century
Description	-	This silk patka is in mauve colour and consists of zari flower creeper designs.

Serial No.	-	72
Show-case No. & M.No.	-	(8) - (125-XXV)
Fabric	-	Silk (Brocade)
Specific Type	-	Patka
School/Place	-	Benaras
Period	-	Early 19th century
Description	-	This brocade patka consists of an attached border.

Serial No.	-	73
Show-case No. & M.No.	-	(8) - (102-XXV)
Fabric	-	Mixed (Brocade)
Specific Type	-	Tash
School/Place	-	India
Period	-	19th century
Description	-	This silver brocade fabric consists of floral and turanj design.

Serial No.	-	74
Show-case No. & M.No.	-	(9) - (75-XXV)

Fabric	-	Silk
Specific Type	-	Sari
School/Place	-	Benaras
Period	-	19th century
Description	-	The dark brown coloured sari consists of zari disc pattern.
Serial No.	-	75
Show-case No. & M.No.	-	(9) - (93-XXV)
Fabric	-	Silk
Specific Type	-	Cloth
School/Place	-	Benaras
Period	-	19th century
Description	-	This orange coloured silk cloth consists of square panels in zari.
Serial No.	-	76
Show-case No. & M.No.	-	(9) - (209-XXV)
Fabric	-	Mixed
Specific Type	-	Cloth
School/Place	-	India
Period	-	Early 20th century
Description	-	This mixed fabric is yellow coloured with diamond and triangle zari design.
Serial No.	-	77
Show-case No. & M.No.	-	(10) - (64-56)
Fabric	-	Silk
Specific Type	-	Sari
School/Place	-	Gujarat
Period	-	19th century
Description	-	This is a maroon colour sari with black flowers from a place called patola in Gujarat.
Serial No.	-	78
Show-case No. & M.No.	-	(10) - (24-XXV)
Fabric	-	Mixed
Specific Type	-	Jamdani
School/Place	-	Benaras Region
Period	-	19th century
Description	-	This jamdani consists of zari work all over.
Serial No.	-	79
Show-case No. & M.No.	-	(10) - (58-XXV)
Fabric	-	Cotton
Specific Type	-	Kamarbandh

School/Place	-	India
Period	-	18th century
Description	-	This cotton kamarbandh is in orange colour having flower pattern.
Serial No.	-	80
Show-case No. & M.No.	-	(10) - (3-XXV)
Fabric	-	Silk
Specific Type	-	Patka
School/Place	-	Kashmir
Period	-	19th century
Description	-	This orange coloured patka consists of flower stalk pattern in embroidery.
Serial No.	-	81
Show-case No. & M.No.	-	(10) - (46/2-XXIV)
Fabric	-	Silk (Brocade)
Specific Type	-	Tray Cover
School/Place	-	India
Period	-	19th century
Description	-	This brocade is depicted with floral pattern in silk and silver thread.
Serial No.	-	82
Show-case No. & M.No.	-	(11) - (131-XXV)
Fabric	-	Mixed
Specific Type	-	Himru Cloth
School/Place	-	India
Period	-	19th century
Description	-	This mixed fabric is pink in colour and consists of leaf and flower pattern.
Serial No.	-	83
Show-case No. & M.No.	-	(11) - (91-XXV)
Fabric	-	Mixed
Specific Type	-	Kimkhob
School/Place	-	India
Period	-	19th century
Description	-	This green kimkhob consists of scale panels in zari.
Serial No.	-	84
Show-case No. & M.No.	-	(11) - (2-XXV)
Fabric	-	Mixed
Specific Type	-	Himru
School/Place	-	India
Period	-	Late 19th century

Description	-	This mixed fabric is mauve coloured with yellow flower design.
Serial No.	-	85
Show-case No. & M.No.	-	(11) - (212-XXV)
Fabric	-	Mixed (Brocade)
Specific Type	-	Cloth
School/Place	-	India
Period	-	Early 19th century
Description	-	This brocade is in pink colour with mango designs and embroidered with green silk dots.
Serial No.	-	86
Show-case No. & M.No.	-	(11) - (185-XXV)
Fabric	-	Mixed
Specific Type	-	Dupatta
School/Place	-	Benaras
Period	-	19th century
Description	-	This is a plain red dupatta.
Serial No.	-	87
Show-case No. & M.No.	-	(11) - (195-XXV)
Fabric	-	Mixed
Specific Type	-	Dupatta
School/Place	-	Benaras
Period	-	19th century
Description	-	This is a dark red dupatta with a plain body.
Serial No.	-	88
Show-case No. & M.No.	-	(11) - (60-XXV)
Fabric	-	Mixed
Specific Type	-	Odhni
School/Place	-	Benaras
Period	-	19th century
Description	-	This is a purple odhni cloth.
Serial No.	-	89
Show-case No. & M.No.	-	(11) - (181-XXV)
Fabric	-	Mixed
Specific Type	-	Dupatta
School/Place	-	Benaras
Period	-	19th century
Description	-	This is also an odhni cloth.
Serial No.	-	90
Show-case No. & M.No.	-	(11) - (62-XXV)

Fabric	- Mixed
Specific Type	- Odhni
School/Place	- Benaras
Period	- 19th century
Description	- This is also a odhni cloth.
Serial No.	- 91
Show-case No. & M.No.	- (11) - (65-XXV)
Fabric	- Mixed
Specific Type	- Odhni
School/Place	- Benaras
Period	- 19th century
Description	- This is an odhni cloth.
Serial No.	- 92
Show-case No. & M.No.	- (11) - (27-XXV)
Fabric	- Silk
Specific Type	- Patka
School/Place	- India
Period	- 19th century
Description	- The colour of this silk patka is pink.
Serial No.	- 93
Show-case No. & M.No.	- (11) - (61-XXV)
Fabric	- Mixed
Specific Type	- Odhni
School/Place	- Benaras
Period	- 19th century
Description	- This is a green, mixed fabric with a plain body.
Serial No.	- 94
Show-case No. & M.No.	- (11) - (182-XXV)
Fabric	- Mixed (Brocade)
Specific Type	- Odhni
School/Place	- Benaras
Period	- 19th century
Description	- This zari (silver) brocade consists of flower - creeper pattern.
Serial No.	- 95
Show-case No. & M.No.	- (12) - (208-XXV)
Fabric	- Silk
Specific Type	- Durri
School/Place	- India
Period	- Early 19th century

Description	-	The durri is printed with flower creeper design on a green base.
Serial No.	-	96
Show-case No. & M.No.	-	(12) - (7-XXII)
Fabric	-	Cotton
Specific Type	-	Curtain
School/Place	-	South India
Period	-	18th century
Description	-	This is a red curtain printed with flower creeper design.
Serial No.	-	97 (Plate 11)
Show-case No. & M.No.	-	(12) - (63-60)
Fabric	-	Cotton
Specific Type	-	Patachitra
School/Place	-	Nathdwara, Rajasthan
Period	-	19th century
Description	-	The singhasan type Patachitra from Nathdwara depicts Hindu mythological scenes in panels showing Gopis, cows and peacocks.
Serial No.	-	98
Show-case No. & M.No.	-	(12) - (63-85)
Fabric	-	Cotton
Specific Type	-	Pichchwai
School/Place	-	Nathdwara, Rajasthan
Period	-	Late 17th century
Description	-	This Pichchwai is from Nathdwara in Rajasthan, a centre of Srinathji cult. This is a famous centre for the production of Pichchwai's. This Pichchwai on display consists of a painting of four Gopis with cows in foreground.
Serial No.	-	99
Show-case No. & M.No.	-	(12) - (24-XL)
Fabric	-	Cotton
Specific Type	-	Cotton/Curtain
School/Place	-	India
Period	-	20th century
Description	-	The red Kalamkari cloth is painted with turanj border flower and creeper design and a medallion in the centre.
Serial No.	-	100
Show-case No. & M.No.	-	(12) - (27-XVI)

Fabric	- Cotton
Specific Type	- Cloth
School/Place	- Kashmir
Period	- 20th century
Description	- This is a printed prayer cloth showing flowers and a medallion in the centre.
Serial No.	- 101
Show-case No. & M.No.	- (12) - (63-65)
Fabric	- Cotton
Specific Type	- Round Cloth
School/Place	- Kalamkari-Machilipatnam
Period	- 19th century
Description	- This round cloth panel is painted with leaves and floral designs.
Serial No.	- 102
Show-case No. & M.No.	- (12) - (62-33-2)
Fabric	- Cotton
Specific Type	- Cover
School/Place	- Kalamkari-Machilipatnam
Period	- 19th century
Description	- The Kalamkari cover from Machilipatnam consists of floral design and turanj pattern.
Serial No.	- 103
Show-case No. & M.No.	- (12) - (79-48)
Fabric	- Cotton-Muslin
Specific Type	- Patka
School/Place	- Benaras
Period	- Late 19th century
Description	- This muslin patka on display is woven with zari thread with animal motifs in the central panel.
Serial No.	- 104 (Plate 12)
Show-case No. & M.No.	- (13) - (53-XXIV)
Fabric	- Cotton-Muslin
Specific Type	- Jamdani & Patka
School/Place	- India
Period	- 19th century
Description	- This jamdani on display is in maroon colour with a patka in karchobi pattern with zari work.
Serial No.	- 105
Show-case No. & M.No.	- (13) - (65-XXIV)
Fabric	- Cotton-Muslin

Specific Type	-	Angarkha & Patka
School/Place	-	India
Period	-	19th century
Description	-	This white muslin angarkha consists of Kamdani work and has a zari bordered patka.
Serial No.	-	106
Show-case No. & M.No.	-	(13) - (62-50)
Fabric	-	Mixed
Specific Type	-	Choga
School/Place	-	Benaras
Period	-	Mid 19th century
Description	-	This costume on display is in maroon colour. It is brocaded with zari all over.
Serial No.	-	107
Show-case No. & M.No.	-	(13) - (83-XXIV)
Fabric	-	Cotton-Muslin
Specific Type	-	Angarkha with Patka
School/Place	-	Dacca
Period	-	18th century
Description	-	This set of costume on display is from Dacca and the fabric is the famous Dacca Muslin.
Serial No.	-	108
Show-case No. & M.No.	-	63-86
Fabric	-	Cotton
Specific Type	-	Cloth
School/Place	-	Deccan
Period	-	18th century
Description	-	The cloth panel consists of a painting depicting Gopis plucking flowers.
Serial No.	-	109
Show-case No. & M.No.	-	80-39
Fabric	-	Cotton
Specific Type	-	Pichchwai
School/Place	-	Rajasthan
Period	-	19th century
Description	-	The scene painted on this Pichchwai consists of Krishna and gopis.
Serial No.	-	110 (Plate 13)
Show-case No. & M.No.	-	216-CSI
Fabric	-	Cotton

Specific Type	-	Curtain
School/Place	-	Kalamkari-Palakollu
Period	-	19th century
Description	-	The curtain is depicted with an episode from Ramayana.
Serial No.	-	111
Show-case No. & M.No.	-	1-XLII
Fabric	-	Cotton
Specific Type	-	Curtain
School/Place	-	Kalamkari-Machilipatnam
Period	-	19th century
Description	-	This curtain from Machilipatnam is painted with an episode from Mahabharata.
Serial No.	-	112
Show-case No. & M.No.	-	73-87
Fabric	-	Cotton
Specific Type	-	Patachitra
School/Place	-	Telangana region, A.P.
Period	-	Early 18th century
Description	-	This patachitra is painted with legends of Hindu Gods.
Serial No.	-	113
Show-case No. & M.No.	-	87-9
Fabric	-	Cotton
Specific Type	-	Patachitra
School/Place	-	Telangana Region, A.P.
Period	-	19th century
Description	-	This patachitra is also painted with legends of Hindu Gods.
Serial No.	-	114
Show-case No. & M.No.	-	64-82
Fabric	-	Cotton
Specific Type	-	Cloth
School/Place	-	Nathdwara, Rajasthan
Period	-	Late 19th century
Description	-	The cloth consists of a painting depicting the Rasleela.
Serial No.	-	115
Show-case No. & M.No.	-	64-81
Fabric	-	Cotton
Specific Type	-	Cloth
School/Place	-	Nathdwara, Rajasthan

Period	-	Late 19th century
Description	-	The painted panel depicts the scene of Krishna with Gopis.
Serial No.	-	116
Show-case No. & M.No.	-	62-51
Fabric	-	Cotton
Specific Type	-	Curtain
School/Place	-	Kalamkari-Palakollu, A.P.
Period	-	Date given as 1840 A.D.
Description	-	The kalamkari curtain depicts an episode from the Sivapurana.
Serial No.	-	117
Show-case No. & M.No.	-	19-XLII
Fabric	-	Cotton
Specific Type	-	Pichchwai/Patachitra
School/Place	-	Rajasthan
Period	-	19th century
Description	-	The pichchwai consists of a scene of Gopis and cowherd.
Serial No.	-	118
Show-case No. & M.No.	-	74-67
Fabric	-	Cotton
Specific Type	-	Pichchwai
School/Place	-	Deccan
Period	-	18th century
Description	-	This pichchwai consists of a scene of Gopis and cowherd.
Serial No.	-	119
Show-case No. & M.No.	-	215-CSI
Fabric	-	Cotton
Specific Type	-	Curtain
School/Place	-	Kalamkari-Palakollu, A.P.
Period	-	19th century
Description	-	The kalamkari curtain is painted with an episode from the Mahabharata.
Serial No.	-	120 (Plate 14)
Show-case No. & M.No.	-	63-55
Fabric	-	Cotton
Specific Type	-	Curtain
School/Place	-	Kalamkari-Kalahasti

Period - Early 19th century
Description - The painted curtain is depicted with a scene from the Ramayana.

II. STATE MUSEUM, HYDERABAD

It is a matter of pride that the State Museum possesses a wide variety of textiles belonging to different art traditions from different parts of the country and also from abroad. The total collection of textiles in the State Museum is 944 pieces. The collection comprises printed, painted and embroidered specimens, besides the rich traditional costumes of the Nizams i.e., Asaf Jahi Times. The collection also includes some of the most aesthetic Holy banners of Tibet known as "Thangkas". Of the several varieties of textiles available in the State Museum only rare specimens have been taken up for the study. The total number of textiles studied under each fabric is :

(A)	Cotton	-	48
(B)	Silk	-	07
(C)	Woollen	-	01
(D)	Mixed	-	04
(E)	Others	-	14

These include shawls, sarees, turbans, patkas; Furnishing materials like bedspreads, curtains, carpets, decorative cloth pieces, saddle cloths; Kalamkari cloths with floral and mythological scenes, temple screens and hangings, prayer cloths and dastarkhans besides the Tibetan Thangkas, Lahore cloth paintings etc. The costumes comprise chogas and official flags of the erstwhile Nizams.

A chronological classification and details of the textiles and costumes is as follows :

Late 16th century	-	S.No. 1
17th century A.D.	-	S.No. 2 to 20
Late 17th cntury	-	S.No. 21 to 29
18th century A.D.	-	S.No. 30 to 34
Late 18th century	-	S.No. 35 to 39
19th century A.D.	-	S.No. 40 to 50
Late 19th century	-	S.No. 51 and 52
20th century	-	S.No. 53 to 57

The following is the detailed study of each object :

Serial No. - 1 (Plate 17)
Museum No. - 3691
Fabric Material - Cotton-Muslin
Specific Type - Kalamkari Curtain
Place - Gujarat
Period - Late 16th century
Measurements - 120 cms x 170 cms
Description - This cotton "chintz" curtain is printed with "shikargah" scene. The big central leaf called Pandu, embellished with floral motifs with stambhas on either side.

Serial No.	-	2
Museum No.	-	3849
Fabric Material	-	Cotton with Silk border and lining
Specific Type	-	Thangka
Place	-	Tibet
Period	-	17th century A.D.
Measurements	-	58 x 80 cms
Description	-	This hand-painted Tibetan banner has the figure of Bodhisattva in the centre represented with eight hands and several heads, seated on bull.
Serial No.	-	3
Museum No.	-	3850
Fabric Material	-	Cotton with Silk border and lining
Specific Type	-	Thangka
Place	-	Tibet
Period	-	17th century A.D.
Measurements	-	60 x 114 cms
Description	-	The central figure of this Thangka is Buddha along with the figures of devotees in meditation.
Serial No.	-	4
Museum No.	-	3851
Fabric Material	-	Cotton with Silk border and lining
Specific Type	-	Thangka
Place	-	Tibet
Period	-	17th century A.D.
Measurements	-	72 x 130 cms
Description	-	Same as Serial No. 3
Serial No.	-	5
Museum No.	-	3852
Fabric Material	-	Cotton with Silk border and lining
Specific Type	-	Thangka
Place	-	Tibet
Period	-	17th century A.D.
Measurements	-	40 x 60 cms
Description	-	Figures faded away
Serial No.	-	6
Museum No.	-	3853
Fabric Material	-	Cotton with Silk border and lining
Specific Type	-	Thangka
Place	-	Tibet
Period	-	17th century A.D.

Measurements	-	68 x 130 cms
Description	-	Handpainted Tibetan banner is represented with the figure of Buddha in the centre with small human figures on top and bottom.
Serial No.	-	7
Museum No.	-	3854
Fabric Material	-	Cotton with Silk border and lining
Specific Type	-	Thangka
Place	-	Tibet
Period	-	17th century A.D.
Measurements	-	78 x 132 cms
Description	-	Figures not clear
Serial No.	-	8
Museum No.	-	875
Fabric Material	-	Cotton
Specific Type	-	Cloth Painting
Place	-	Tibet
Period	-	17th century A.D.
Measurements	-	60 x 105 cms
Description	-	Painting on cotton cloth with an eight-handed Buddhist deity in the centre and small human figures all around.
Serial No.	-	9
Museum No.	-	877
Fabric Material	-	Cotton
Specific Type	-	Cloth Painting
Place	-	Tibet
Period	-	17th century A.D.
Measurements	-	53 x 86 cms
Description	-	Same as S.No. 8
Serial No.	-	10
Museum No.	-	878
Fabric Material	-	Cotton
Specific Type	-	Cloth Painting
Place	-	Tibet
Period	-	17th century A.D.
Measurements	-	54 x 100 cms
Description	-	Same as S.No. 9
Serial No.	-	11
Museum No.	-	880
Fabric Material	-	Cotton

Specific Type - Cloth Painting
Place - Tibet
Period - 17th century A.D.
Measurements - 68 x 125 cms
Description - Same as S.No. 10

Serial No. - 12
Museum No. - 881
Fabric Material - Cotton
Specific Type - Painting Cloth
Place - Tibet
Period - 17th century A.D.
Measurements - 46 x 95 cms
Description - Cloth painted with a four-armed deity in the centre and small human figures all around.

Serial No. - 13
Museum No. - 882
Fabric Material - Cotton
Specific Type - Painting Cloth
Place - Tibet
Period - 17th century A.D.
Measurements - 50 x 82 cms
Description - Same as S.No. 12

Serial No. - 14
Museum No. - 2599
Fabric Material - Silk (Brocade)
Specific Type - Patka
Place - Hyderabad
Period - 17th century A.D.
Measurements - 48 x 240 cms
Description - The silk patka has floral patterns in silver zari.

Serial No. - 15 (Plate 18)
Museum No. - 2600
Fabric Material - Silk (Brocade)
Specific Type - Patka
Place - Hyderabad
Period - 17th century A.D.
Measurements - 50 x 225 cms
Description - Same as S.No. 14

Serial No. - 16
Museum No. - 2605

Fabric Material	-	Cotton
Specific Type	-	Saree
Place	-	Chanderi
Period	-	17th century A.D.
Measurements	-	385 x 134 cms
Description	-	This is a saree from Chanderi in bottle green colour with zari Border.

Serial No.	-	17
Museum No.	-	6494
Fabric Material	-	Cotton
Specific Type	-	Wall Hanging
Place	-	—
Period	-	17th century A.D.
Measurements	-	400 x 234 cms
Description	-	This wall hanging is hand painted with human figures.

Serial No.	-	18
Museum No.	-	6502
Fabric Material	-	Mixed
Specific Type	-	Choga
Place	-	Hyderabad
Period	-	17th century A.D.
Measurements	-	120 cms. long
Description	-	This brocaded tunic with golden zari background is designed with floral patterns.

Serial No.	-	19
Museum No.	-	6503
Fabric Material	-	Mixed
Specific Type	-	Choga
Place	-	Hyderabad
Period	-	17th century A.D.
Measurements	-	127 cms long
Description	-	Same as S.No. 18

Serial No.	-	20
Museum No.	-	8689
Fabric Material	-	Cotton
Specific Type	-	Dupatta
Place	-	—
Period	-	17th century A.D.
Measurements	-	725 x 107 cms
Description	-	The creame colour dupatta has zari border on both ends.

Serial No.	-	21
Museum No.	-	80-18/19
Fabric Material	-	Cotton
Specific Type	-	Wall Hanging
Place	-	—
Period	-	Late 17th century
Measurements	-	—
Description	-	This pair of wall-hanging has floral patterns in silver zari.

Serial No.	-	22
Museum No.	-	2500
Fabric Material	-	Cotton with silk border and lining
Specific Type	-	Thangka
Place	-	Tibet
Period	-	Late 17th century
Measurements	-	70 x 110 cms
Description	-	Faded away

Serial No.	-	23
Museum No.	-	2501
Fabric Material	-	Cotton with silk border and lining
Specific Type	-	Thangka
Place	-	Tibet
Period	-	Late 17th century
Measurements	-	70 x 114 cms
Description	-	Figures faded away

Serial No.	-	24
Museum No.	-	2502
Fabric Material	-	Cotton with silk border and lining
Specific Type	-	Thangka
Place	-	Tibet
Period	-	Late 17th century
Measurements	-	60 x 118 cms
Description	-	The thangka is depicted with the figure of Buddha in the centre surrounded by disciples.

Serial No.	-	25
Museum No.	-	2503
Fabric Material	-	Cotton with silk border and lining
Specific Type	-	Thangka
Place	-	Tibet
Period	-	Late 17th century
Measurements	-	59 x 110 cms
Description	-	Same as S.No. 24

Serial No. - 26
Museum No. - 2504
Fabric Material - Cotton with silk border and lining
Specific Type - Thangka
Place - Tibet
Period - Late 17th century
Measurements - 60 x 110 cms
Description - This thangka is depicted with Buddha as the central figure surrounded by dhyani Buddhas.

Serial No. - 27
Museum No. - 2606
Fabric Material - Cotton
Specific Type - Painted Cloth
Place - Rajputana
Period - Late 17th century
Measurements - 192 x 160 cms
Description - This cotton pichchwai is painted with various episodes from Life of Lord Krishna in separate compartments all along the border. In the centre Krishna is seen as Govardhana Giridhari raising mount Govardhana as an umbrella to protect his followers from the rainstorms unleashed by the fury of God Indra. This form of Krishna is commonly known as Shri-Nathji by the followers of the Vallabha sect.

Serial No. - 28
Museum No. - 8755
Fabric Material - Silk
Specific Type - Carpet-Tapestry
Place - Kashmir
Period - Late 17th century
Measurements - 260 x 540 cms
Description - This beautiful carpet from Kashmir consists of a green background embroidered with yellow and red floral patterns.

Serial No. - 29 (Plate 19)
Museum No. - 7107
Fabric Material - Silk
Specific Type - Carpet Tapestry/Wall Hanging
Place - Kashmir
Period - Late 17th century
Measurements - 213 x 446 cms
Description - Another massive carpet also used as wall hanging consists of

a dark brown background embroidered with geometric designs in silk and zari and has an embossed floral border in red colour.

Serial No.	-	30
Museum No.	-	2497
Fabric Material	-	Cotton with silk border and lining
Specific Type	-	Thangka
Place	-	Tibet
Period	-	18th century
Measurements	-	58 x 105 cms
Description	-	Hand painted Buddhist banner showing the devotees in meditation.

Serial No.	-	31
Museum No.	-	2498
Fabric Material	-	Cotton with silk border and lining
Specific Type	-	Thangka
Place	-	Tibet
Period	-	18th century A.D.
Measurements	-	53 x 97 cms
Description	-	This thangka is depicted with Buddha Figure in the centre surrounded by monks.

Serial No.	-	32
Museum No.	-	2499
Fabric Material	-	Cotton with silk border and lining
Specific Type	-	Thangka
Place	-	Tibet
Period	-	18th century A.D.
Measurements	-	68 x 120 cms
Description	-	Same as S.No. 31

Serial No.	-	33
Museum No.	-	5276
Fabric Material	-	Woollen
Specific Type	-	Shawl
Place	-	—
Period	-	18th century A.D.
Measurements	-	48 x 112 cms
Description	-	Half white colour shawl with red border having floral designs.

Serial No.	-	34
Museum No.	-	76-28
Fabric Material	-	Cotton/Curtain
Specific Type	-	Painted Cloth/Kalamkari

Place	-	Masulipatnam
Period	-	18th century A.D.
Measurements	-	—
Description	-	This painted cloth contains episodes from Mahabharata.

Serial No.	-	35
Museum No.	-	2615
Fabric Material	-	Cotton
Specific Type	-	Kalamkari Curtain
Place	-	Masulipatnam
Period	-	Late 18th century
Measurements	-	140 x 168 cms
Description	-	This kalamkari curtain from Masulipatnam is black printed with figures of animals and human beings.

Serial No.	-	36
Museum No.	-	2616
Fabric Material	-	Cotton
Specific Type	-	Kalamkari Curtain
Place	-	Masulipatnam
Period	-	Late 18th century
Measurements	-	195 x 280 cms
Description	-	Another kalamkari curtain from Masulipatnam contains floral patterns in red and black colours.

Serial No.	-	37
Museum No.	-	2649
Fabric Material	-	Cotton
Specific Type	-	Kalamkari table cloth
Place	-	Masulipatnam
Period	-	Late 18th century
Measurements	-	102 cms diameter
Description	-	This kalamkari table cloth from Masulipatnam is round and printed with floral designs.

Serial No.	-	38
Museum No.	-	6488
Fabric Material	-	Silk
Specific Type	-	Saree (Patola)
Place	-	Murshidabad
Period	-	Late 18th century
Measurements	-	110 x 440 cms
Description	-	A patola silk saree from Murshidabad in double weave in red, white and black colours having elephants, parrots and floral patterns.

Serial No. - 39
Museum No. - 6867
Fabric Material - Cotton
Specific Type - Kalamkari Screen
Place - Jaipur
Period - Late 18th century
Measurements - 205 x 140 cms
Description - This cotton kalamkari screen from Jaipur is printed with Rajasthani floral patterns.

Serial No. - 40
Museum No. - 1031
Fabric Material - Cotton
Specific Type - Curtain Cloth
Place - Lahore
Period - 19th century A.D.
Measurements - 110 x 180 cms
Description - This curtain like cloth from Lahore has a brown background printed with floral designs in an arch. The prints are locally known as Lahore prints.

Serial No. - 41 (Plate 20)
Museum No. - 1032
Fabric Material - Cotton
Specific Type - Wall-hanging
Place - Lahore
Period - 19th century A.D.
Measurements - 100 x 80 cms
Description - A very beautiful piece from Lahore, printed with a peacock in the centre and a floral border all around. This brown colour vertical cloth piece is probably a wall-hanging.

Serial No. - 42
Museum No. - 1033
Fabric Material - Cotton
Specific Type - Square Cloth Panel
Place - Lahore
Period - 19th century A.D.
Measurements - —
Description - This square cloth panel from Lahore is depicted with floral patterns.

Serial No. - 43 (Plate 21)
Museum No. - 1035
Fabric Material - Cotton

Specific Type	-	Square Cloth Panel
Place	-	Lahore
Period	-	19th century A.D.
Measurements	-	84 x 90 cms
Description	-	This square cloth panel from Lahore is depicted with floral patterns with beautifully printed fish and birds in between the floral border.

Serial No.	-	44 (Plate 22)
Museum No.	-	1042
Fabric Material	-	Cotton
Specific Type	-	Rumal
Place	-	Lahore
Period	-	19th century A.D.
Measurements	-	40 x 38 cms
Description	-	A mustard colour rumal from Lahore having the "Turanj" patterns in the four corners and has a floral border.

Serial No.	-	45
Museum No.	-	1045
Fabric Material	-	Cotton
Specific Type	-	Curtain - Afridi Work
Place	-	North-West Frontier Province
Period	-	19th century A.D.
Measurements	-	100 x 272 cms
Description	-	This cotton curtain from North-West Frontier Province was purchased from Peshawar and is an interesting piece. The light blue colour cotton curtain is printed with several compartments each containing floral designs of different style locally known as Afridi work. It is bounded by a floral border in red colour.

Serial No.	-	46
Museum No.	-	1050-51
Fabric Material	-	Cotton
Specific Type	-	Kalamkari Bedspread
Place	-	Masulipatnam
Period	-	19th century A.D.
Measurements	-	118 x 200 cms
Description	-	A pair of kalamkari bedspreads from Masulipatnam are painted with figures of human beings, birds (peacocks) and animals (camels).

Serial No.	-	47
Museum No.	-	2353

Fabric Material	-	Cotton
Specific Type	-	Kalamkari Temple hanging
Place	-	Kalahasti
Period	-	19th century A.D.
Measurements	-	68 x 156 cms
Description	-	This kalamkari temple hanging from Kalahasti is painted with figures of Rama, Sita, Hanuman and other figures.

Serial No.	-	48 (Plates 16 and 23)
Museum No.	-	2354
Fabric Material	-	Cotton
Specific Type	-	Kalamkari Curtain
Place	-	Kalahasti
Period	-	19th century A.D.
Measurements	-	60 x 86 cms
Description	-	This cotton kalamkari curtain from Kalahasti is painted with the story of Gajendra Moksha. This episode is painted according to original Bhagavata where Gajendra in distress cries for the help of Vishnu. Vishnu who is in Vaikuntha with his consort and Garuda, his vehicle, departs to save Gajendra on the Garuda with his consort. This is depicted in two scenes. The Gajendra moksha episode by following the original Bhagavata is depicted on a 9th century sculpture in the Alampur museum of Mahbubnagar district in Andhra Pradesh.

Serial No.	-	49
Museum No.	-	3697
Fabric Material	-	Cotton
Specific Type	-	Kalamkari Dastarkhan
Place	-	Masulipatnam
Period	-	19th century A.D.
Measurements	-	97 x 124 cms
Description	-	This dastarkhan from Masulipatnam is block printed with floral and creeper design. There are some poetic verses (ashar) all along the border in black. It would be interesting to mention that the system of spreading the dastarkhan during dinner was in vogue in Hyderabad upto 1655 A.D.

Serial No.	-	50
Museum No.	-	3698
Fabric Material	-	Cotton
Specific Type	-	Kalamkari Janemaz
Place	-	Masulipatnam
Period	-	19th century A.D.

Measurements	-	142 x 88 cms
Description	-	This is a vertical cloth panel used as a prayer mat. The distinguishing feature is the design. It depicts a cusped arch with minarets.

Serial No.	-	51 (Plate 24)
Museum No.	-	87-44
Fabric Material	-	Cotton
Specific Type	-	Kalamkari Temple hanging
Place	-	Kalahasti
Period	-	Late 19th century A.D.
Measurements	-	Length 5 mts - 83 cms Width 2 mts - 43 cms
Description	-	This is a massive kalamkari temple hanging from Kalahasti depicted with various episodes from Ramayana. The central panel depicts "Seetha Rama Kalyanam". It is a piece of excellent workmanship and the figures are painted artistically.

Serial No.	-	52
Museum No.	-	1048-49
Fabric Material	-	Cotton "Chintz" muslin
Specific Type	-	A pair of Sangnair "Chintz"
Place	-	Jaipur
Period	-	Late 19th century
Measurements	-	125 x 240 cms
Description	-	This pair of cotton chintz from Jaipur is block printed with flora and fauna.

Serial No.	-	53 (Plate 27)
Museum No.	-	4779
Fabric Material	-	Cotton
Specific Type	-	Asafia Flag
Place	-	Hyderabad
Period	-	20th century
Measurements	-	5.5 x 3 ft.
Description	-	This is the flag of the erstwhile Hyderabad State. It was predominantly yellow with green and white stripes. The dastar (headgear) was above the shield in the centre. The dastar had on the top the inscription *Al-Azmat lillah* (all greatness of God). Inside the shield was inscribed the dynasty *Asaf Jah Nizam ul-mulk* and at the bottom is contained the name of the seventh Nizam, Ya Osman. There are various versions regarding the origin of the colour of the flag, circles etc. Since a yellow cloth was wrapped round the head of Nizam-ul-

mulk by the famous saint, Hazrat Nizamuddin Aulia at Delhi, yellow became the official colour of the state and the flag. Another version is that the white circle in the centre signified the moon (*Qamar* in Arabic means the moon) as the name of the first Nizam was Qamaruddin. The yellow Asaf Jahi flag was the official flag of the state till 1948 and fluttered over King Kothi till the Nizam's death on 24th February, 1967.

Serial No.	-	54
Museum No.	-	1561
Fabric Material	-	Mixed
Specific Type	-	Sherwani
Place	-	Hyderabad
Period	-	20th century A.D.
Measurements	-	107 cms in length
Description	-	This red sherwani is decorated with silver zari work.

Serial No.	-	55
Museum No.	-	5611
Fabric Material	-	Cotton
Specific Type	-	Kalamkari Temple hanging
Place	-	Kalahasti
Period	-	20th century
Measurements	-	—
Description	-	This cotton kalamkari temple hanging is painted with the mythological scenes.

Serial No.	-	56 (Plate 25)
Museum No.	-	5613
Fabric Material	-	Cotton
Specific Type	-	Phulkari Cloth
Place	-	Punjab
Period	-	20th century
Measurements	-	75 x 300 cms
Description	-	This phulkari from Punjab has a blue background embroidered with floral patterns and mirror work.

Serial No.	-	57 (Plate 26)
Museum No.	-	6490
Fabric Material	-	Cotton
Specific Type	-	Phulkari cloth
Place	-	Punjab
Period	-	20th century
Measurements	-	142 x 244 cms
Description	-	This red colour phulkari is embroidered in white.

Besides the above fabrics the following are undated old specimens which have been taken up for a meticulous study.

Serial No.	-	58
Museum No.	-	80-20
Fabric Material	-	Cotton
Specific Type	-	Embroidered cloth piece
Place	-	Deccan
Period	-	Old Piece
Measurements	-	—
Description	-	Embroidered with flower-leaf pattern.

Serial No.	-	59
Museum No.	-	80-21
Fabric Material	-	Cotton
Specific Type	-	Painted cloth
Place	-	—
Period	-	Old Piece
Measurements	-	68 x 45 cms.
Description	-	This painted cloth depicts the scene of a lady seeing a deer.

Serial No.	-	60
Museum No.	-	87-56
Fabric Material	-	Mixed
Specific Type	-	Brocade
Place	-	—
Period	-	Old Piece
Measurements	-	—
Description		Zari work in silver.

Serial No.	-	61
Museum No.	-	1027
Fabric Material	-	Cotton
Specific Type	-	Bedsheet
Place	-	Lucknow
Period	-	Old Piece
Measurements	-	—
Description	-	This cotton bedsheet from Lucknow is printed with floral patterns. It is a well preserved old piece.

Serial No.	-	62
Museum No.	-	1044
Fabric Material	-	Cotton muslin
Specific Type	-	Printed cloth
Place	-	—

Period	-	Old Piece
Measurements	-	—
Description	-	This cotton muslin with white background is printed with the "shikargah" scene.
Serial No.	-	63
Museum No.	-	1047
Fabric Material	-	Silk
Specific Type	-	Saddle Cloth
Place	-	Bokharo
Period	-	Old Piece
Measurements	-	—
Description	-	This saddle cloth in silk is from Bokharo.
Serial No.	-	64
Museum No.	-	2000
Fabric Material	-	Cotton
Specific Type	-	Screen
Place	-	Not Mentioned
Period	-	Old Piece
Measurements	-	—
Description	-	This cotton screen is printed with human figures in dance pose.
Serial No.	-	65 (Plate 28 and 29)
Museum No.	-	2571
Fabric Material	-	Silk
Specific Type	-	Jamewar
Place	-	Bengal/Kashmir
Period	-	Old piece
Measurements	-	92 x 128 cms
Description	-	This handwoven silk Jamewar from Bengal/Kashmir has two sides. One side of the cloth is in grey colour with small white flowers. The other side has a light green background woven with red flowers.
Serial No.	-	66
Museum No.	-	2610
Fabric Material	-	Cotton and wool
Specific Type	-	Carpet
Place	-	—
Period	-	Old Piece
Measurements	-	450 x 306 cms
Description	-	This carpet or spread is woven with three compartments in the shape of arches within which are the designs of a vase with flowers. The compartments are bounded by a floral border.

Serial No.	-	67
Museum No.	-	2650
Fabric Material	-	Cotton
Specific Type	-	Painted cloth
Place	-	—
Period	-	Old Piece
Measurements	-	—
Description	-	Round cloth painted with floral designs.

Serial No.	-	68
Museum No.	-	3449
Fabric Material	-	Cotton
Specific Type	-	Curtain
Place	-	Rajasthan
Period	-	Old Piece
Measurements	-	204 x 288 cms
Description	-	This cotton curtain from Rajasthan is printed with flora, fauna and female dancing figures.

Serial No.	-	69
Museum No.	-	5273
Fabric Material	-	Cotton muslin
Specific Type	-	Turban
Place	-	Not mentioned
Period	-	Old Piece
Measurements	-	—
Description	-	This is a white cotton turban, made of fine muslin.

Serial No.	-	70
Museum No.	-	5614
Fabric Material	-	Cotton
Specific Type	-	Block printed cloth panel
Place	-	Not mentioned
Period	-	Old Piece
Measurements	-	186 x 130 cms
Description	-	This cotton cloth is printed with Female figures in the border.

Serial No.	-	71
Museum No.	-	6782
Fabric Material	-	Cotton
Specific Type	-	Pichchwai (wall hanging)
Place	-	Rajasthan
Period	-	Old Piece
Measurements	-	—
Description	-	This wall-hanging is printed/painted with 'Rasleela' scene.

Serial No.	-	72
Museum No.	-	6788
Fabric Material	-	Cotton
Specific Type	-	Pichchwai
Place	-	Rajasthan
Period	-	Old Piece
Measurements	-	—
Description	-	Printed with human figures.

Serial No.	-	73
Museum No.	-	6791
Fabric Material	-	Cotton
Specific Type	-	Temple screen
Place	-	Chennai
Period	-	Old Piece
Measurements	-	—
Description	-	This screen from Chennai (Madras) has decorative motifs in needle work.

Serial No.	-	74
Museum No.	-	6868-69
Fabric Material	-	Cotton
Specific Type	-	Kalamkari cloth panels
Place	-	Masulipatnam
Period	-	Old Pieces
Measurements	-	—
Description	-	Two identical Kalamkari painted cloth panels from Masulipatnam are hand block printed and painted with flora and fauna.

CHAPTER - III

FABRICS

The following is a Material-wise classification of Textiles displayed in the Salar Jung Museum and also the Textiles in possession of the State Museum, Hyderabad :

1. SALAR JUNG MUSEUM, HYDERABAD

1.	No. of Exhibits in R.No. 6 of the Museum	107
2.	No. of Exhibits in R.No. 3 of the Museum	13
	Total No. of Exhibits on Display	**120**

A. Cotton

	Material	*Number*
1.	Cottons	34
2.	Muslins	4
		38

B. Silk

	Material	*Number*
1.	Silk	16

C. Woollen

	Material	*Number*
1.	Woollens	10

D. Mixed Fabrics

	Material	*Number*
1.	Mixed Fabrics	50

E. Miscellaneous

	Material	*Number*
1.	Other Materials	6

II. STATE MUSEUM, HYDERABAD

Total number of textile for which details could be obtained is seventy four.

A. Cotton

	Material	*Number*
1.	Cottons	44
2.	Muslins	4
		48

B. Silk

	Material	*Number*
1.	Silk	7

C. Woollen

	Material	*Number*
1.	Woollens	1

D. Mixed Fabrics

	Material	*Number*
1.	Mixed Fabrics	4

E. Miscellaneous

	Material	*Number*
1.	Other Material	14

A fabric literally means 'Cloth'. The making of cloth is regarded as one of the earliest industries for the reason that clothes along with food have always been the basic needs of man since the dawn of early civilization. From being an essential part of the personality of an individual, a group or a whole society, the use of fabrics was extended to decorating the home and also for festive occasions. The wealth of a person as well as the cultural traditions of the people are conveyed through its textiles. The textiles and costumes from the very beginning have played a very important role in expressing the advancement of material culture of the human race. In India, too, the textile art is very old.[1] Textiles or Fabrics are classified into different materials. Cotton, Silk, Woollen and some of the Mixed Fabrics are covered in the study.

A. Cotton

Cotton Chemistry

Cotton is a vegetable-seed fibre. Botonically, the fibres are the protective covering of the seeds in the cotton plant Gassypium. This is a shrub which grows from four to six feet high.

Chemical Properties

When dry, cotton fibre is almost entirely made up of cellulose. In addition to cellulose it contains small amounts of protein, pectin, wax, ash, organic acids and pigment.

Physical Characteristics

Strength - The tensile strength of the cotton fibre is greater when wet than when dry.

Absorbancy - It has remarkable capacities for absorbing moisture. It can absorb and release perspiration quickly, has great affinity for dyestuffs and bleaches excellently to a clear white.

Head Action - It can be sterilized at boiling temperatures without disintegration. It withstands dry heat upto 248^0 F and can be ironed at relatively high temperatures without damage.

Washability - Because it is stronger wet than dry it stands up well under the rigors of repeated launderings. It also has good resistance to alkalies.

Durability - It stands up well in abrasion tests, and a fibre can be bent as many as 50,000 times without rupture.[2]

Cotton spinning and cotton weaving go back to the earliest recorded days of our civilization. Cotton fabrics have been found in the exavations at Mohenjodaro, the ruins of which are attributed to the 3rd millennium B.C. The discovery of cotton was a break-through in the history of textile development.[3] Apart from being durable and washable, cotton had elegance and grace compared to skins and barks previously used for clothing.

The sanskrit word for cotton is *Karpasa*. The word *Sindhu* apparently meaning cotton, indicates that the Sindh Valley was the land of origin of this basic staple and that the cotton products were being exported even in those remote days.[4]

Literally, cotton is a fabric made from the fibres which cloth the seeds of the cotton plant. The discovery of many spindles and spindle whorls (or *Takkis*) at Mohenjodaro reveal that spinning of cotton was very common.[5] In the *Rig Veda*, Day and Night are said to spread light and darkness over the earth as weavers throw a shuttle on the loom. Cotton cultivation and its use in weaving originated in India.[6] Cotton fibres have been spun into threads and woven into textiles since very early times, probably c. 3000 B.C. in India where cotton was cultivated by c 1000 B.C.[7]

The woven fabric has always been of great importance as an expression of the tradition and culture of the people. In many parts of the country the first cotton wrap from newly harvested cotton is blessed, by the local priest.[8] The weaving together of the warp and weft into a fabric has been a source of wonder for the human mind.

According to Arrian, Indian cottons were whiter and brighter than were those of any other region, and according to Lucian, the 'Indian Fabrics' were lighter and softer than the Greek.[9]

India produces an enormous variety of cotton handloom products. The handloom industry is an age-old source of livelihood for millions of people in our country. Handloom is a household industry, spread throughout the country. Its charm and uniqueness has attracted every strata of our society. History has it that hand weaving was in existence in India for over 5000 years from now.[10] India, from the most ancient times, till the beginning of the 18th century was the supplier of cotton of rare excellence to all civilized countries in the world. Not only was the Handloom

Industry meeting the entire cloth requirements of the Nation, but also exporting huge quantities abroad earning wealth to the country, besides name and fame.[11] Thirty four cotton Textile objects on display in the Salar Jung Museum and Forty Four cotton textile pieces from the State Museum, Hyderabad are studied.

Varieties of Cotton

Muslin

Cotton weave is the special product of India and the country is famous throughout the world for fine cotton muslins, known by such poetic names as "woven air", 'running water' and 'evening dew'.[12] Muslin represents the highest achievement of the cotton-weaving industry in India. Muslin is a variety of plain material woven all over the country. No other country has been able to excel the great beauty and extreme delicacy of these fine textures. Plain muslin was at one time produced everywhere in the north as well as in the south; but the most famous weaves are those of Dacca which have won unmatched reputation all over the World.[13] The finest muslin of Dacca was called *mulmul khas*. The fineness and delicacy of this variety made it suitable only for regal attire. India as the home of fine muslins has always displayed the most dexterously spun fabrics on her transparent cloth as wonderful.[14] Bana compares it to the light skin of the snake which rustles in the wind.[15] In the *Jatakas*, the muslin of Benaras was so famous that it could not absorb oil. It is said the body of Buddha was shrouded in this cloth.[16]

Some of the muslins, it is said, were absolutely fabulous. It is believed that fine weaving passed on from India to Assyria, Egypt and through the phoenicians into Southern Europe.[17] The muslins of Dacca have rightly been famous for centuries and justly considered the masterpieces of the Indian weaver in cotton, for the extreme delicacy and the great beauty of the Dacca muslins of old stand unsurpassed.[18] The excellence of the fabric depends upon its length and the number of threads in the warp as compared to its weight, the greater the length and the number of threads and the lower the weight, the better the fabric. A 15 yard piece weighed only 900 grains. A wet muslin piece laid on grass would be invisible and because it was indistinguishable from the evening dew, it was named *Shabnam* - The evening dew. Another was called *Abe-Rawan* or running water, as it became invisible in water. (Indian Handicrafts - Kamaladevi Chattopadhyaya - p.31). It is only in a moist atmosphere that such fine threads can be spun. Therefore, the spinning is done during the rainy season, or early in the morning and in the evening, sometimes over a shallow vessel of water. Otherwise the delicate threads are liable to snap, either while laying the warp or on the loom.[19] The fine Indian muslin was called 'ventus textiles' or 'nebula'.[20] Indian muslin was famous in Rome.[21] According to Periplus, the best muslin was known as *monache*. Sindh and Masulipatnam exported Muslin to countries like Egypt and Arabia. But it is said that the best muslin was manufactured at Varanasi or Dacca.[22]

The manufacture of cloth like other manufactured articles received special importance during the Mauryan period.[23] It is said that women were employed for spinning and weaving as was the practice in the Vedic Age. The *Arthasastra* records the fame of eastern Bengal and the Gangetic delta for their famous white and soft muslins. In the scythian are muslins of the best quality known as Gangetica were exported in large quantities to the Roman empire mostly in the first century

A.D. During the reign of the Guptas there was great improvement in textile craft.[24] During the 10th century the textiles of Gujarat were carried to Egypt by Arab traders. During the Sultanate period the textile industry developed along traditional lines through the guilds and crafts of the village communities and of urban areas without the guidance and patronage of the rulers. It was in the 16th century when the art and crafts of weavers burst forth with renewed vigour under Mughal patronage. During the Mughal period, the most important industry was the manufacture of cotton cloth. As already mentioned the best and finest cloth made of cotton came from Dacca. It is said that a whole piece of muslin manufactured for the use of royalty was packed in a hollow bamboo tube lacquered and gilded for despatching to Delhi or Agra.[25]

The celebrated Dacca Muslins are now a thing of the past. The chief centres of muslin manufactures today are Benaras, Dacca, Hyderabad, Jaipur, Mysore, Kotah, Gwalior Arni, Indore, Madurai and Tanjore.[26] Four Muslins from the Salar Jung Museum and four from the State Museum, Hyderabad are studied.

Muslin is called by different names. Such as :

Shabnam	-	evening dew
Abe-Rawan	-	running water
Bafthma	-	Woven air
Mal Mal Khas	-	King's Muslin
Sarbati	-	Sweet as sherbet

The *dorias* or striped muslins are a speciality of Dacca, Gwalior, Hyderabad and Nagpur. From here as well as Nellore come the *checkered* or charkana, and the figures jamdani from Dacca. The flowered; muslins have small flower sprays worked on them with unequalled delicacy of touch, all arranged in a many diverse ways but always producing a most delightful effect. Mention may be made of the embroidered muslins of Calcutta known as Chikan, the painted muslins of Tiruchirapalli and the gold and silver fabrics of Gujarat, Jaipur, Hyderabad and the Deccan plateau.[27]

The *Mal Mal Khas* or 'King's muslin' could be made in lengths of 10 yards and one yard in width, containing from 1000 to 1800 threads in the wrap. These could only be made during the rainy season, the moisture in the air allowing the very fine thread to be woven, and would take a weaver almost five months to complete.[28]

More beautiful still are the *figured muslins - The jamdanis* - The jamdani may be called a product of the shuttle in which the designs are inserted by the hand during the process of weaving, and producing the effect of embroidery. As in tapestry weaving, small bobbins or shuttles filled with coloured gold or silver threads, are passed through the warp, the weaver producing the exquisite designs by the skilful use of the bobbins in the course of intricate weaving. No wonder the best jamdanis of old are today prized heirlooms of many a Bengali family.[29] Of the four muslin pieces in the Salar Jung Museum S.N. 104 (M.No.53-XXIV) is a lone Jamdani with Patka on show.

Dr. James Taylor describes the process of weaving these figured fabrics.[30] "In manufacturing figured fabrics two weavers sit at the looms. They place the pattern drawn on paper, below the warp, and arrange along the track of the woof a number of cut threads equal to the flowers or parts of the design intended to be made and then, with two small fine pointed bamboo sticks, they draw each of these threads between as many threads of the warp as may be equal to the width of the figure which is to be formed. When all the threads have been brought between the warp they are drawn close by a stroke of the lay. The shuttle is then passed by one of the weavers through the shed, and the weft having been driven home, it is returned by the other weaver. The weavers resume their work with their pointed bamboo sticks and repeat the operations with the lay and shuttle in the manner above described, observing each time to pass the flower threads between a greater or less number of the threads of the warp, in proportion to the size of the design to be formed."

The following is a much simpler description of the *Daccai Jamdani Saris* by Pupul Jayakar[31] - "The long warp threads being arranged, the weaving is begun as in the case of an ordinary cloth, and a pattern of embroidery drawn on paper is pinned beneath. As the weaving goes on, the workman continually raises the paper pattern to ascertain if his woof has approached closely to where any flower or other figure has to be embroidered, and when the exact place is reached, he takes his needle (i.e., a bamboo splinter) and as each woof thread passes through the pattern, he sews down the intersected portion of it, and so continues until it is completed. Two persons generally work together at a piece of Jamdani, by which a great saving of time is effected."

The most remarkable thing about these fabrics is unquestionably their rich variety of designs, some of which are clearly of Persian origin.[32] The cone *(kalka)* locally known as 'turanj' is very largely used at the corners and the field is covered with small sprays *(buti)* of flowers like the Jasmine *(chameli)*, the marigold *(genda)* and the chrysanthemum *(gul dandi)*. In the sprays, patterns of small circular dots *(chanda)*, stars *(tara)*, betel leaves *(pan)* and bouquets of flowers *(tora)* are also used. Jalar is the name for the jamdani which has floral designs arranged in a network covering the entire field, and jamewar for the weave with a pattern of large flowers arranged in rows. Occasionally, the sprays are grouped in diagonal lines and are then known as *tircha buti*. Jamdanis with running floral patterns covering the entire field are known as *phulwaris* and those with sprays of flowers linked together as *panna-hazara*. Usually threads of two different textures are used to pick out the patterns. Some times gold and silver threads, and more rarely coloured threads, are used to pick out the design in order to impart greater relief to the surface. The borders usually consist of broad bands of running floral scrolls. Occasionally figure subjects such as horse-riders *(ghorsawar)*, hamsas and mayura-pankhis (boats shaped like peacocks) gliding down a stream are introduced in the borders. S.No.62 (M.No.1044) of the State Museum is decorated with Hunting Scene, S.No.103 (M.No.79-48) of the Salar Jung Museum is cotton muslin patka bears animal and floral motifs in the central panel.

It should be emphasized that the patterns in Dacca Jamdanis are, like brocades, distinct from and supplementary to those where the weft is thrown on its surface by means of bamboo sticks. Although the term brocade is usually applied to silk fabrics alone, the figures and flowered Jamdanis of Dacca may also be so described since the technique used is so strikingly similar.[33]

B. Silk

Definition

"Silk is a fibrous substance produced by many insects, principally in the form of a cocoon or covering within which the creatures are enclosed and protected during the period of their principal transformation, the webs and nets etc., formed by spiders are also of silk. But the fibres used for manufacturing purposes are exclusively produced by the mulberry silk moth of China, Bombyx mori, and few other moths closely allied to that insect". *Encyclopaedia Britannica.*

Silk Chemistry

Obtained from the Central Silk Board, Bombay.

Structure of Silk Fibre

The silk fibre is a complex substance mainly composed of fibroin and sericin, containing a small quantity of pigments which is mainly found in the sericin, waxes, sugars and in organic substances which are found in both sericin and fibroin.

Characteristics of Silk Fibre

There are many kinds of fibres different from each other in various points but those issued for clothing have some common characters. These common characters are :

(a) The fibre is fine and long.

(b) The molecule forming a fibre is fine and long. The molecules in a fibre are arranged in order, and in some fibre they are arranged as if they are twisted. These conditions resemble a thread which is composed of orderly arranged, or twisted fibres.

(c) The fibre is suitable in tenacity, elongation and elasticity. These three points are the requirements from view points of the morphology of fibres, arrangement of molecules and use of fibres, respectively. However, many differences are also noticed between different kind of fibres. These are :

  (a) Differences in the structure and length of each molecule in fibres.

  (b) Differences in the arrangement of molecules in a fibre.

  (c) Differences of the structure and form occurred during the formation of fibres.

(d) Differences of the secondary constituents other than the main components of a fibre. Such structural elements as mentioned above are different according to the kinds of fibres, and it may be said that the characteristics peculiar to each fibre are determined in close relation with these minute factors in structure. We have many artificial fibres today in addition to natural fibres as clothing material. Different kinds of fibres, even if they resemble externally, have different structures, and their uses are determined by these structural peculiarities. Consumption of fibres is increasing year by year for various uses. But, there is no fibre which can be used for every purpose.

The silk fibre has such characteristics as follows in comparison with other fibres.

(a) The silk fibre is composed of proteins peculiar to it. Protein is a naturally existing highly polymerised substance.

(b) Cocoon filaments and raw silk consist of two different proteins, that is, fibroin and sericin. Such a dualistic structure cannot be seen in other fibres.

(c) The silk fibre has characteristic elasticity.

(d) The silk fibre is high in affinity to dyestuffs, so it can be dyed beautifully.
(e) The silk fibre is excellent in lustre and hardness which are important characteristics for clothing fibres.
(f) The silk fabric keeps warmth well, absorbs or releases moisture moderately. It is also easy for sewing, light in weight and not easily crumpled. These are all desirable characters for clothing.

The silk fibre can be used for fabrics and knittings, because it has excellent characteristics for the purpose. However, owing to recent development of artificial fibres, some of these, characteristics now can not be exclusive ones for the silk fibre. For instance, silk was the only long fibre formerly, but now we can make long fibres artificially. This is a remarkable fact which shows that competitors of silk have grown strong enough now. Furthermore, the yellowing, less resistance to rubbing, knots and lousiness are weak points of the silk fibre which should be improved to meet the demands of market. The main object of sericulture and filature is to produce silk for the use of the clothing. And among many studies on the production and use of silk, improvement of silk-worm varieties and of techniques of filatures, knitting and weaving are carried out to better every characteristic of silk, while modifications of the minute structure of silk by treatment with synthetic resins or chemical aim to improve the nature of silk physico-chemically.[34]

Indian Silk fabrics held a place of pride in almost all countries of the world. Silk has dominated the history of clothing, through the centuries, both by its eminent qualities of strength and durability. Silk clothing is considered as the identity of affluence and gentility. Its rare qualities lend an air of unmatched graciousness and beauty. Silk combines fineness of texture with astonishing durability. Silk fabrics, if properly treated, will last for years. There are many homes in India where Silk brocades and sarees are handed down from mother to daughter and from generation to generation and are preserved as family heirlooms. A silk fabric is a must for an Indian family used during all festive and religious occasions. Silks are preferred on marriage and other happy occasions all over the world. Therefore, silk is used for the finest apparel, pleasing elites of the society for ages and prized to this day for its luxurious qualities. Silk fabrics are the most perfect products of art that human skill and fancy have ever created in textile fibres.[35]

Silk has been the special product of China, but it is possible that it was introduced into India long before the age of the epics.[36] However, there are no records to confirm when silk from China reached India.[37] Silk-weaving is mentioned in Indian texts at least as early as the third century B.C.[38]. Varanasi or Benaras is one of the most important silk-weaving centres.[39] Originally it lay in the midst of a cotton growing area and was famous for its cotton weaves. In Pali literature, the city referred to as Kasi, is mentioned as a reputed centre of textile manufacture. Certain generic terms came to be known for particular Silks, such as *Kasi Kuttami*" and *Kasiya*. Patanjali in the second century B.C. refers to *Kasiya* as a textile superior to those woven in Mathura.

The literary meaning of silk is, "A natural fibre spun into a cocoon by the larva of the mulberry silk-moth of China, the Bombyx mori, first used for textiles of a very early period in China. The oldest surviving fragments date from c. 1000 B.C. and reveal fairly advanced knowledge of the technique of weaving. Silk was exported to Europe from the time of the Han

Dynasty (220 B.C. - 202 B.C.). The Romans imported not only silk textiles but also silk yarn"[40]. The present work studies twenty two Silk textiles. Of them sixteen belong to the Salar Jung Museum and seven from the State Museum, Hyderabad.

The breed of silk worm, Bombyx Mori which provides most of the world's silk, feeds on mulberry leaves for the five weeks of its life. Then it spins round itself a cocoon of fine silk thread which is eventually reeled into skeins, ready for manufacture into yarns for fabrics and stockings.[41] Silk is acclaimed as the queen of fibres. The charm, beauty and elegance of silk fabrics are beyond reach of any other textile fibre. No fibre gives such lasting satisfaction to the human heart as silk.[42] No other fibre whether of vegetable origin or animal or man-made can compete with silk in strength, resilience, lustre, drape, warmth, handle and durability. Commercially silk is classified into 'Wild-silk is the product of silk-worms which feed on the leaves of various trees and plants growing in the forests. True silk is the product of the mulberry silk-worms.

The mention of silk and silk-worms is also found in the early epics of India.[44] Though silk is recognised as the special product of China, it is possible that it was introduced into India long before the epic period. The Indians turned this material into a highly specialised craft and Indian silk products were praised greatly in other countries until recent times. The silks studied in the present work belong to different regions across our country-from Kashmir to Kanchipuram. They also include places from China, the original home of silk and also from Bokharo.

Silk-weaving is mentioned in Indian texts at least as early as the third century B.C. but the implication is that only the wild silks, were known at this time. There is no evidence that the cultivated silk-worm reached India from China before the first centuries of our era.[45]

The *Kalika Purana* calls the silk from cocoons of various kinds of silk-worm as 'Kosaja'.[46] Early Hindu literature speak of mulberry silk as an imported article and further that it is not until comparatively modern times that we have direct indications of a fairly extensive silk production in India.[47] As it seems evident from *Periplus of the Erythrean Sea* that, silks were exported to the land of the Nile, perhaps from Bengal.

C. Wool

Wool Chemistry : From the Encyclopaedia of textiles by the Editors of American fabrics magazine.

Definition : Wool is the fibre of a living animal. It forms the protective covering of the sheep, insulating it against both heat and cold and keeping its body temperature even.

Chemically wool is described as a protein called keratin. Keratin contains 18% of the known amino acids which are basic to living matter and is built up through a complex molecular structure known as a polypeptide chain. In general composition it is some what similar to human hair.

Chemical Properties

It is composed of Carbon, Hydrogen, Oxygen, Nitrogen and Sulphur.

Wool is a living fibre. Under the Microscope it shows three distinct parts :

1. Epidermis

2. Cortex
3. Medulla

Physical Characteristics

Dimensions : From 1 to 14 inches or more in length.

Strength : Can be bent 20,000 times without breaking. Extremely flexible.

Elasticity : Can be stretched to an additional 25% to 35% of its own length without breaking.

Resiliency : Natural elastic recovery causes it to original position after being stretched or creased. It is therefore wrinkle-resistant.

Crimp : Natural crimp or waviness of the fibre gives it bulk, enables it to trap air and so provide insulation.

Absorbancy : Will absorb upto 30% of its weight in moisture without feeling damp. This explains its affinity for dyes. Perspiration is absorbed and so does not cool the body by evaporation.

Heat Action : Begins to disintegrate at 212^0 F.

Characteristics of Woollen Fabrics

1. Woollen fabrics generally have a soft feel and fine surface.
2. They have little shine, or sheen.
3. Woollen do not hold a crease well.
4. Their tensile strength is relatively low.
5. As a rule, woollens use less expensive yarns than worsteds.
6. Woollens take great depth of colour in dyeing.
7. Woollens are generally heavier and bulkier than worsteds.
8. Woollens are more suited to casual fashions.[48]

Wool is an important raw material. The use of wool for woven textiles, has a very ancient history in India. The Vedas refer to woollen yarn as covering for the body.[49]

A fine variety of wool is called "PASHM". Wool is known as *Urna* in the Epics. Kambala was a texture of fine wools.[50] The *Arthasastra* also mentions wool *(urna)* among other materials employed for spinning.[51] The Sabha Parva mentions the places from which wool and woollen goods, skins etc., came to India.[52] The wool of the shawlgoat fetched a very high price in ancient times. For fine texture and softness, no Asiatic wool could compare with the Pashm wool of the shawlgoat of Kashmir, Bhutan, Tibet and the Northern face of the Himalayas.[53] For woollen clothes of all varieties the term Kambala is used in Buddhist literature. In the days of the *Samhitas* woollen clothing was in practise. Woollen Blankets and cloaks are often mentioned in the *Samhitas*.[54]

The *Arthasastra* mentions a large number of wild animals from which furs and skins were obtained. The generic name of all woollen goods was Rankava and sometimes, Lomaja (Woollen and hairy).[55]

Wool takes a very subordinate position among the art crafts of India. This proceeds from two circumstances, viz., its unsuitability as a material of clothing to the climatic conditions of the greater part of this country and its very perishable nature, when subject to the conditions that prevail in India.[56]

Floor-Coverings and Pile Carpets

Floor coverings have always been an important part of the interior of a home in India, the use of furniture being very limited. The homes of the rich and the poor used until recently a minimum of furniture and most of the living was done at the floor-level.[57] Pile-carpets were probably introduced into India from Iran. The earliest reference to them is found in the 15th century, when their export to other countries was mentioned in the travelogies of the period.[58]

All writers seem to agree in thinking that pile carpet weaving, like a great many more of the arts of India, came from Persia, though it is quite probable that India possessed a carpet-weaving industry of its own long interior to the advent of any Persian influence. There are methods and designs met with here and there, in the Indian carpet trade, that are very possibly indigeneous and which have greatly tended to bring about the peculiarities that allow of Indian carpets being at once recognised from those of other countries.[59] Detailed references to the pile-carpet industry are found in *Ain-i-Akbari*. During the Mughal period, this industry flourished in Agra, Delhi, Lahore, as also in the Deccan.[60] The emperors of Delhi and Agra encouraged the art and kept their State weavers. The weavers produced marvellous carpets. Moreover it is fairly certain that at many important centres of administration all over the Empire, there were state factories, though the *Ain-i-Akbari* has little to say about them.[61]

There are two centres in Andhra Pradesh noted for the woollen pile carpet industry, viz., *Eluru* and *Warangal*.[62] The pile-carpet industry for which Warangal earned a name appears to have been introduced by some Muslim Nawabs of the place. The industry was obviously borrowed from Persia. The industry with its technique already developed in Persia, appears to have been introduced into Warangal for no other reason but the availability of the chief raw material, namely, wool, at the local tanneries and the demand for the pile carpets from the luxury loving nawabs. It would appear that originally, mostly prayer carpets of size 4' x 2' and a set design were being manufactured here and supplied to the Muslim nobility. It is, however, not clear when exactly the woollen pile-carpets started to be manufactured at Warangal.[63] It is well known that during the time of the Golconda rulers there was free intercourse of trade and culture between this part of the country and the middle Eastern countries. The old traditional designs of the Warangal carpets go by the following names:[64]

1. Hashim Khani
2. Delhi Khani
3. Teerandas Khani
4. Mahbub Khani
5. Thotti Designs

These are all Persian designs and said to consume a lot of labour. It has to be mentioned here that the designs are not standarised. Generally, the designs which could be manufactured are too numerous, but they bear no individual names as such. No particular care is bestowed at Warangal for naming the carpets by their designs. One carpet in rags bearing No. 930 from the State Museum is from Persia.

Eluru is renowned for its woollen pile carpet industry.[65] The industry here seems to be quite thriving and certainly the decadence of the Industry which was observed in Warangal is not found here. Even so the industry in this city also seems to have had its own ups and downs. There is no recorded evidence about how and when the carpet industry came to be started in this city. It is obvious that this industry was not indigenous but introduced from outside. It is believed to be the result of the Mughal rule over this part of the country. The local workmen relate that about 500 years ago (the actual period seems to be somewhat of a guess-work, it might be even later) the Mughal army happened to encamp in the area over the ground close to the present Railway Station near Lakshmivarapupeta, which is even now referred to as a military camping ground. It is said that a couple of Persians amongst the camping troops stayed back in Tangellamudi on the outskirts, which now forms part of the city, and they settled down there having married from amongst the local Muslim families. It seems that, these two persons knew the art of Persians' carpet weaving. In the olden days, in this part of the country, the local weavers and dyers were specialists in vegetable dyeing. This seemed to have encouraged the new settlers to start a pile carpet industry using the local dyes.[66] There were also some shepherd families in the neighbourhood and apparently the wool was also readily available. Tangellamudi has come to be predominantly populated by Muslim community. These people ran tanneries also. Thus the environment and the availability of raw material seem to have proved propitious for the development of the pile carpet industry. Soon, most of the Muslim families in the area picked up this craft. Most of the individual families had small looms in homes and with the simple technique involved and the limited implements needed it was not found too difficult for the local workmen to develop skill in the making of the pile carpets, which soon won a wide reputation.[67]

Shawls of Kashmir

The Salar Jung Museum has a rich collection of Kashmir Shawls of the 18th and 19th centuries. Of all the Indian textiles none excells the beauty of colour, texture and design of the richly patterned shawls of Kashmir, Shawl-weaving is common in the north-western part of India, but it is in Kashmir that it has reached its highest development.[68] Sometimes the Himroo cloth is also used as shawls.[69] The shawls of Kashmir have been known for the past many centuries.[70] In *Ain-I-Akbari*, Abul Fazl while enumerating the shawls of the emperor, mentions Kashmir 'Shawl'. He also writes about how the Emperor Akbar was fascinated by the shawls and the favour extended by him to the woollen industry of Kashmir. Much more has been written on these fascinating fabrics.

The shawl is a fabric woven from the under-fleece of species of a goat, a fine variety of wool called *pashm*.[71] The Kashmir shawls were popular not only on account of the warmth they provided but also on account of their rich decorative designs which was either woven or embroidered. Sometimes the two processes are combined. Whether woven or embroidered it is almost always made of small pieces separately prepared and joined together so skilfully that the seams are scarcely visible.[72] The old shawls represent the highest form of craftsmanship combined with incredible patience, untiring labour and an aesthetic sense of a very high order.

Assigning, choosing the colour scheme, and plotting the weave according to the needs of the design require a greater gift than that of a mere craftsman.[73]

The shawls exhibit an extensive variety of patterns and forms. The relief is often densely packed with minute floral and foliar motifs, and occasionally figure subjects and architectural settings are also introduced. The colours are chosen to harmonize with the ground and with one another so that the finer examples of this work look like paintings. Sometimes, the pattern is worked in such a manner as to appear the same on both sides, and when this is so the fabric is called a Dorukka.[74]

The innumerable shades of colours one finds in pieces of Kashmir embroidery, support the theory that the riot of colours which go to the making of the gorgeous sunsets, the azure mountains, the sparkling lakes and the variegated flowers and birds, have left their indelible mark on the minds of the workers. The designs are evenly balanced. In designing a motif, the artist naturally selects from his own surroundings a subject which he can present compellingly and attractively, with an eye on colour and line. The main motifs in the designs are flowers, leaves, fruits and birds, among birds, the most popular are the parrot, the magpie, the kingfisher, the woodpecker and the canary. Butterfly designs are also to be found, but flower and foliage are the dominant motifs. The popularly known shawl pattern is supposed to have been inspired by the cypress cone, almond or river loop in Kashmir and dominates most designs in some form or other.[75]

D. Mixed Fabrics

(i) Himroo
(ii) Mashru

(i) Himroo : Mixed fabrics with patterns brocaded in silk over the surface are known as Himrus.[76] Aurangabad is the home town of Himroo. The origin of Himroo at Aurangabad was linked with the advent of Muslim rule in Southern India. In 1656 A.D. Emperor Aurangzeb established his Deccan head quarters at Aurangabad, and along with the centre of administration the weavers must have had settled at that town. Thus, Himroo is an antique and traditional art that came down from generations and generations of artisans in Bharat.[77]

The Himroo is a notable production of flowered textiles and employs a variety of patterns. The cloth is an extra weft figuring fabric having a solid coloured ground decorated with motifs of flowers, leaves, birds, fruits etc.[78] The ground is of uniform colour, usually green, blue, pale slate, maroon or scarlet and the patterns are picked out in pink, red, yellow and white, according to the ground colour. One of the most popular designs is known as the 'Jangla', a foliage motif which is repeated. The 'Sia Jangla' consists of a hanging creeper with flowers and foliage mixed up with miniature cones. Other characteristic floral designs are known as 'Uda Jaldar' and 'Suk Monibel', the patterns of the latter being usually arranged within stripes. On the right surface, the execution is very neat and the rich and warm tones of colour lend these textiles an unusual degree of elegance and grace.[79]

Besides the above mentioned patterns, the various designs that can be woven on the Himroo cloth include the following:[80]

(a) Plain designs composed of lines.

(b) Geometrical designs consisting of circles, diamonds, hexagons etc.

(c) Designs of fruits like mango, pomegranate, almond etc.

(d) Flowers like rose, jasmine, lotus, chameli, etc.

(e) Flowering creepers with leaves and stems connecting one another to form a running creeper.

(f) Birds and animals like double bird, elephant etc.

(ii) Mashru : Another kind of tie-dye cloth is the Mashru. This is woven out of mixed silk and cotton, in which the warp only is tie-dyed before weaving with characteristic patterns of wavy lines. The technique of weaving this cloth is however, similar to that of Himroo cloth. Himroo and Mashru consist of the cotton yarn for warp and silk for weft and are woven in spotted, striped or elaborate floral designs on satin ground. In the Himroo, the cotton from which it is woven is spun so as to form a soft thick fabric that feels like wool. Sometimes woollen yarns are mixed with cotton. It is brocaded in silk threads which form loose masses on the under-surface because they are clumsily behind from one point to the other in the design.

The term 'Mashru' is derived from *'Shara'* which means the "law". The material is so called because the mixture of cotton with it makes the silk permissible to wear when praying.[81]

Himroo and Mashru make attractive tunics and vests for men and blouses or coats for ladies. The Himrus were originally used as "Achkans" by the nobles of Golconda court, due to its excellence in quality, texture and attractive designs.

References

1. Saraswati S.K. *Indian Textiles*, 1961, Faridabad p.1.
2. *Census of India*, 1961, Vol.XX, Part VII-A No.2 "Himachal Pradesh", Delhi, 1968, p.16.
3. Marg Publication, *Maharashtra - Traditions in Art* Vol.XXXVI No.4, p.29.
4. Saraswati, S.K. Op.Cit., 1961, p.1.
5. *Bharatiya Vidya* (Journal) Vol.III, Part-I, p.152.
6. Agnes Geijer, *A History of Textile Art*, London, 1979.
7. *The Penguin Dictionary of Decorative Arts*, p.208.
8. Jasleen Dhamija & Jyotindra Jain (Eds.) *Handwoven Fabrics of India,* p.13.
9. Warmington, *Commerce between the Roman Empire and India,* p.212.
10. Venkateshwara Rao, A. *Handloom Industries in India - A Study*, New Delhi, 1973, p.1
11. Somappa, M. *Textiles & Embroidery*, New Delhi, 1973, p.1. Article, p.76.
12. Saraswati, S.K. Op.Cit., 1961, p.1.
13. Ibid, p.3.
14. Sivaramamurthi, C. *Amaravati Sculptures in the Madras Govt. Museum*, Madras, 77, p.116
15. Ibid, p.116.
16. Moti Chandra, *Trade and Trade Routes in Ancient India*, New Delhi, 1977, p.66.
17. Kamaladevi Chattopadhyay, *Indian Handicrafts*, p.31.

18. Ibid., p.96.
19. Ibid., p.5.
20. Moti Chandra - *Costumes, Textiles, Cosmetics & Coiffure,* Delhi, 1973, p.30.
21. Moti Chandra - Op.Cit., 1973, p.126.
22. Ibid.
23. Biswas, A. *Indian Costumes,* 1985, New Delhi, p.110.
24. Ibid.
25. Ibid.
26. Mehta Rustom, J. *The Handicrafts & Industrial Arts of India*, Bombay, 1960, p.96.
27. Ibid.
28. Ibid, p.97.
29. Ibid.
30. Ibid.
31. Pupul Jayakar, (Ed.) *Textiles & Embroideries of India*. Section-II, Embroideries, p.16.
32. Saraswati, S.K. Op.Cit, 1961.
33. Ibid.
34. Census of India, 1961. Vol.XX, Op.Cit., pp.23-25.
35. Jayanth Kumar G. Parikh. *Silk & Man-made Fibres* (Article - Textiles India, 1956), p.255
36. Saraswati, S.K. Op.Cit., 1961, p.1.
37. Biswas, A. Op.Cit., 1985, p.110.
38. Marg Publications, *Textiles & Embroideries of India*, p.5.
39. Dhamija Jasleen, *Indian Folk Arts & Crafts*, New Delhi, 1970, p.14.
40. The Penguin Dictionary, Op.Cit., p.208
41. Jayanth Kumar G. Parikh, Op.Cit., 1956, p.256.
42. Ibid, p.355.
43. Barua, B.K. *A Cultural History of Assam*, Vol I, Gauhati, 1969, p.142.
44. Saraswati, S.K. Op.Cit., 1961, p.1.
45. Marg Publications, Op.Cit., p.5.
46. Barua, B.K., Op.Cit., 1969, p.142.
47. Sir George Watt. *Indian Art at Delhi*, 1903, Calcutta, p.290.
48. Census of India, 1961. Vol.XX, Op.Cit., pp.20-21.
49. Saraswati, S.K. Op.Cit., 1961, p.2.
50. Barua, B.K. Op.Cit., 1969, p.141.
51. Shama Shastry, R. (Ed.). Op.Cit. (Translated), p.113.
52. Moti Chandra, Op.Cit., 1973, p.16.
53. Ibid, p.31.
54. Ibid.
55. Majumdar, R.C. (Ed.) *The History and Culture of Indian People*, Vol.I, p.393.
56. Brij Bhushan, Jamila. *The Costumes and Textiles of India*, Bombay, p.16.
57. George Watts & Percy Brown. *Arts & Crafts of India*, New Delhi, 1979, p.338.
58. Dhamija, Jasleen, Op.Cit., 1970, p.36.
59. Ibid, p.39.
60. George Watts & Percy Brown, Op.cit., p.425.
61. Dhamija, Jasleen, Op.cit., 1970, p.39.
62. George Watts & Percy Brown, Op.cit., p.426.
63. Census of India, 1961, Vol.II Op.Cit., p.39.

64. Ibid.
65. Ibid, p.72.
66. Ibid.
67. Ibid.
68. Saraswati, S.K. Op.Cit., 1961.
69. Census of India, 1961, Vol.II Op.Cit., p.47.
70. Ibid.
71. Ibid.
72. Ibid.
73. Ibid.
74. Ibid.
75. Ibid.
76. Saraswati, S.K. Op.Cit., 1961.
77. Census of India, 1961, Vol.II Op.Cit., p.47.
78. Ibid.
79. Saraswati, S.K. Op.Cit., 1961.
80. Census of India, 1961, Vol.II Op.Cit., p.47.
81. *Hyderabad. Art Archaeology of Handicrafts*, Article - Handicrafts State by Mahmood Mirza. p.XXXIII.

CHAPTER - IV

TECHNIQUE

Culture and Craft, in India, are closely associated. Hand weaving in our country has truly been termed as an art and craft for it has produced some best known varieties of fabrics which include the Benaras Brocades, the Patolas of Gujarat, the finest Muslins, the beautiful Himroos of Aurangabad, the exquisite Kashmiri shawls and other well-known varieties of other centres. The equipment which assists this synthesis of art and craft is the simple Handloom. There are different kinds of looms and these when classified, form two broad groups - viz., Handlooms and Powerlooms. In the present study we are concerned with only the Handlooms, which are distributed all over India chiefly in the rural parts. The handlooms can be classified either based on the raw material used or on the structure of the loom employed. On the basis of the former, the looms could be classified into four main groups:[1]

a) Looms weaving mainly cotton fabrics.
b) Looms weaving mainly silk and art-silk fabrics.
c) Looms weaving woollen fabrics.
d) Looms engaged in weaving other fibres.

Based on their structure and technique of working, the handlooms could be classified into six main groups:

a) Loin Looms and other primitive or traditional looms.
b) Vertical Looms - such as drugget looms or carpet looms.
c) Pit Looms.
d) Frame Looms.
e) Semi-automatic Looms - "Sley Motion" Type.
f) Semi-Automatic Looms - "Treading" Type.

Early Looms[2]

The earliest evidence of the use of the loom (4400 B.C.) is a representation of a horizontal two bar loom pictured on a pottery dish found at al-Badari, Egypt. In addition to the horizontal two-bar loom, there are two other primitive varieties, the warp-weighed (loom consists of a crossbar supported by two vertical posts) and the vertical two-bar loom. Loom weights have been found at archaeological sites dating from 3000 B.C., but this type of loom might have originated even earlier. The earliest picture of a vertical two-bar loom is from the Egyptian 18th dynasty (1567-1320 B.C.). By about 2500 B.C. a more advanced loom i.e., Horizontal frame loom, was apparently evolving in the far East. The earliest European pictorial record of the horizontal frame loom with a treadle dates from the 13th century, when it appears in a highly developed form, almost certainly introduced from the East. In about 1490 Leonardo da Vince[3] worked out the principle of automatic loom for weaving plain textiles. In 1725 Basile Bouchon in France designed a mechanism to select the cords to be drawn automatically. This was improved upon in 1745 by Jacques de Vancanson whose loom came to be known as the Jacquard Loom. This made possible the weaving of the most elaborate patterns by an operator. The machine was invented in 1801 and eleven thousand of them were in use in France by 1812. It was introduced into England in C 1810. This was later on replaced by the Powerloom.

This chapter is an attempt to examine the various Technical aspects involved in creating the textile materials viz., Cotton, Silk, Woollen and Mixed Fabrics. It also presents a detailed study of the Manufacturing process involved with cloths like the Cotton Muslins, the Kancheepuram Silk Sarees, the Woollen Shawls of Kashmir and the Himroo Fabrics of Aurangabad.

(A) Cotton

Cotton-weaving is so universal that it is difficult to list places where some weaving is not done. India, from the most ancient times, till the beginning of the 18th century, was the supplier of excellent cotton to all civilized countries in the World. The earliest method of preparing cotton fibres for weaving was derived from the ancient India method. The cotton fleece was hand picked and ginned. The cotton fibres were then spun into a thread. This home-spun thread was then woven on handlooms in the house-hold.[4] The cotton in the form of 'Kapas', is cleaned and prepared by the women who spin the yarn. The wool adhering to the seed is carded with the jawbone of the Baolifish. To detach the fibres from the seeds, a small quantity is placed upon a smooth flat board, upon which the spinner rolls an iron pin backward and forward with the hands so as to separate the fibres without crushing the seeds. The cotton is then teased out with a small hand bow formed of a piece of bamboo with two elastic slips of the same material inserted into it and strung with a cord of catgut, silk or of twisted plantain or rattan fibre. Thus reduced to a light, downy fleece the cotton is spread out and wrapped round a thick, wooden roller and on the removal of the latter instrument, it is pressed between two flat boards. It is next rolled round a piece of lacquered reed and lastly is enveloped in the soft and smooth skin of the Cuchia fish which serves as a cover to protect it from dust and from being soiled, while it is held in the hand during the process of spinning.[5]

Spinning Equipment

The spinning apparatus which is usually contained in a small, flat work basket comprises the cylindrical roll of cotton, a delicate iron spindle - no thicker than a needle and a concave piece of shell embedded in clay.

Process of Manufacturing Muslin Cloth

The spinner sitting on a low stool holds the spindle in an inclined position with its point resting in the hollow of the piece of shell and turns in between thumb and forefinger of one hand, while at the same time drawing out the single fibres from the roll of cotton held in the other hand, and twists them into yarn upon the spindle. A certain degree of moisture combined with a temperature of about 82^0 F. is the condition of atmosphere best suited to this operation. Dacca spinners generally work from soon after early dawn till about 9 or 10 O' clock before the rising sun disperses the dew on the grass. When the air is dry, the spinning is done over a shallow vessel of water, the evaporation from which imparts the necessary degree of moisture to the fibres of the cotton. It is said that fabrics made of Dacca yarn were more durable than muslins manufactured by machinery. A half piece of the finest kind took at least six months to make while a whole piece of muslin, inferior in quality, could be made in eight days. After a lengthy process of weaving, for bleaching, fine muslins are steeped in water and are next immersed for some hours in an alkaline lye. They are then spread over the grass and are occasionally sprinkled with water and when half dried are removed to the boiling house to be steamed. The boiler is an earthen vessel having a very wide mouth and capable of containing 8 to 10 gallons of water. It is placed over a small excavation in the ground and built up with clay, so as to form a broad, flat surface round its neck, having at one part a slanting opening or passage leading to the excavation below. A hollow tube or reed fitted with a cup or funnel made of coconut shell serves as a tube through which water is poured into the vessel. The pieces of cloth are twisted into forms of loose bundles and placed upon the broad clay platform, on a level with the boiler. Fire is kindled in the excavation below and as the ebullition of water proceeds the steam rises through the wide mouth of the vessel and diffuses itself through the mass of cloth above, swelling by its high temperature the threads of the latter and allowing the alkali adhering to them to penetrate more completely into their fibres and seize on the colouring matter of the cotton. The operation of steaming is commenced in the evening and allowed to continue all night. Cloths are then removed from the boiler, steeped in alkaline lye and spread over the grass as on the previous day and are again steamed at night. This process is repeated for ten or twelve days, until the pieces of cloth are perfectly bleached. After the last steaming they are steeped in clear, filtered water acidulated with lime juice in proportion of one large lime to each piece of cloth. The ancient mode of packing muslins was to enclose them in hollow joints of bamboo - sufficiently long to contain 22 yards of cloth of one yard width. The greater the length and number of threads and the less the weight, the greater was the value of cloth. Best after Dacca are the muslins of Arnee in Madras.[6] The town of Arni in North Arcot is well known for its fine muslins. Other muslins in, South India, that have a high local fame are Adoni, Kampti, Madura and Tanjore. The Venkatagiri muslin is mostly used for turbans. It is white with gold or coloured band.[7] Besides these, the chief centres of muslin manufacture today are Benaras, Dacca, Hyderabad, Jaipur, Mysore, Kotah, Gwalior and Indore. The Salar Jung Museum displays four muslins S.Nos. 103, 104, 105 and 107 of these S.No. 107 is from Dacca the Angarkha and Patka belongs to the 18th century. Among the collections of State Museum, Hyderabad S.No. 69 M.No. 5273 and S.No. 62 - M.No. 1044 are Muslin cloths. The former is a turban and the latter is a cloth consisting of a hunting scene, datable to the Moghul period. The Indian weaver was an expert of the *'Jamdani'* or the loom figured muslin with the exquisite delicacy of manipulation and their complicated designs. The following is a description of jamdani weaver as given by Taylor[8]. In manufacturing figured muslins two weavers sit at the loom. They place the pattern drawn upon paper below the warp, and range along the track of the woof a number of cut threads equal to the flowers or parts of the designs intended to be made; and then with two small pointed bamboo sticks they draw each of these threads of the warp as may be equal to the width of the figure which is to be formed. When all the threads have been brought between the warp they are drawn close by the stroke of the lay. The shuttle is then passed by one of the weavers through the thread and the weft having been driven home it is returned by the other weaver. The weavers resume their work with their pointed bamboo sticks, shuttle in the manner above described, observing each time to pass the flower threads between a great or less number of the threads to be formed." No wonder the best jamdanis of old are today prize heirlooms of a many a Bengali family. S.No. 104, M.No. 53-XXIV from the Salar Jung's collection is a Jamdani with patka belongs to the 19th century. S.No. 78 - M.No. 24-XXV is also a Jamdani from Benaras region, has zari flowers. This also belongs to the 19th century.

(B) Silk

Silk is also extensively woven in India. Silk is a natural fibre spun into a cocoon by the larva of the mulberry silk-moth of China, the Bombyx mori, first used for textiles at a very early period in China. The oldest surviving fragments date from c. 1000 B.C. and reveal fairly advanced knowledge of the technique of weaving. Silk was exported to Europe from the time of the Han Dynasty (220 B.C. - 202 B.C.). The Romans imported not only Silk textiles but also silk yarn.[9] At what time it came to India, it is not possible to ascertain. But it soon came to be much appreciated and was extensively used by all the rich who could afford it. It was both imported and woven in the country. Silk worms were extensively reared and the silk-weaving of India came to hold a position of the world second only to China.[10] Silk-weaving is mentioned in Indian texts at least as early as the third century B.C., but the implication is that at this time only wild silks were known. There is no evidence that the cultivated silk worm reached India from China before the first centuries of our era.[11]

Wild Silk and True Silk are the two chief varieties of silk found in India. In the first variety i.e., wild silk, India has three well-known indigenous silk-worms, viz., the Tasar, the Muga and the Eri. The first mentioned is widely distributed, being met with in all the lower hill tracts of the great table-land. It has proved intractable or difficult of domestication. The cocoons are simply placed on the jungle trees on which the worm feeds and protected as far as possible from their enemies. Tasar (silk) textiles are usually of a dull or greyish straw colour, when not dyed, and are of a stiff texture. The second insect is confined to Assam and Eastern Bengal, and is more or less domesticated. It feeds on a species of laurel and yields a rich golden coloured silk that is fairly extensively employed in the art crafts of India. The last mentioned insect also exists in a state of semi-domestication. It is reared on the castor oil plant, but the fibre is devoid of the gloss and other properties. It is reared chiefly in Eastern Bengal, Assam and to a certain extent in the United provinces also. True Silk is produced from the Mulberry Silk-worm. Early Hindu literature speak of mulberry silk as an imported article and further that it is not until comparatively modern times that we have direct indications of a fairly extensive silk produced in India. It is possible, that the tasar silk of Northern and Central India and the eri and muga silk of Assam might have been known and manufactured long anterior to the mulberry feeding insect.[12]

The weaving and the spinning of silk is done in the same crude ways as that of cotton but the results produced are magnificent.

The *Spinning apparatus* comprises of a circular bamboo cage, spokes, reels etc. The gathering, spinning and weaving of the wild silks was concentrated in the interior tribal areas. The cloth was woven on primitive bamboo looms.

Spinning

The raw silk is sorted, reeled and twisted by women. It is then dyed by the weaver himself and the part intended for the warp is sent to the warper. To sort and reel the silk, a skein is moistened and thrown round a rough circular bamboo cage. In the centre of the cage is a rod, from each end of this rod are fastened spoke-like pieces of narrow bamboo. The ends of the two sets of spokes are tied together with cords and the skein of silk is thrown over the cords. The woman who reels, sits to the left of the cage and on her right side are two or three reels with long handles and points. The spinning is done by setting the bottom of the central rod of the cage in a porcelain cup or a smooth coconut shell.[13]

Silk Weaving of Kanchipuram

Kanchipuram is a famous centre for its gleaming silks, rich in colour and texture. The silk fabrics of Kanchipuram are as well known, as those of Benaras. The superb nature of the Kanchipuram silk saree have made it a by-word in every household along the length and breadth of India. But unfortunately there is no authentic record to trace the origin of the silk industry in Kanchipuram and it is also surprising that such an important silk weaving centre, Kanchipuram imports the main raw materials, silk and gold lace from Bangalore and Surat respectively.

Origin of the Craft

According to local sources, weavers were originally in the habit of using silks for the borders of cotton sarees produced by them. Later on, they started producing sarees known as Koravai sarees of cotton in which a mixture of silk and cotton formed the basic components and by a gradual process of evolution, cotton yard was given up completely and weavers in Kanchipuram took to the production of pure silk fabrics.

Other sources[14] claims that these weavers originally belonged to Kaveripoompattinam, which was submerged in the second century A.D., might have migrated to Kanchipuram and introduced silk weaving there. As Kanchipuram was the capital of the Pallavas and came under the sway of the later Cholas, it is likely these weavers took to silk weaving to cater to the needs of the royal family. Another version states that these weavers known as Saliyars claim to be descendants of the sage Mrikanda, the weaver of the Gods and their original home appears to have been the Andhra Country from where a section of the Saliyars was invited by the Chola King, Raja Raja I, after the union of the Eastern Chalukyas and Chola dynasties. Since the Pallava Empire extended upto the banks of the river Krishna and Kanchipuram was under the sway of the later Cholas, this explanation for the origin of the craft here may perhaps be the more authentic one.

Looms Used[15]

In Kanchipuram, in addition to the production of silk fabrics, a number of looms are engaged in the production of cotton and other fabrics. The cotton cloth is woven on Fly Shuttle Looms and the bulk of the silk fabrics are woven on throw shuttle looms. The silk weavers at Kanchipuram form a separate category of weavers there and they would not ever attempt to produce cotton fabrics as they consider it below their dignity.

Techniques of Production[16]

Tools and Equipment

The throw shuttle looms consist of the following parts :

1. Slay
2. Treadles
3. Reed
4. Healds
5. Warp beam
6. Cloth beam
7. Shuttle with pirn
8. Lease rods

The most usual variety of fabric produced in Kanchipuram is known as Koravai or solid border. In this fabric, the weft threads do not enter into the borders. In the case of fabrics having borders on both sides at least 3 shuttles are utilised, while in the case of fabrics having border on one side two shuttles are required.

The Loom

The reed through which the warp passes is fixed to the 'Slay'. It is manually operated by hand. The Treadles are attached to the Healds and in conjunction with the Lease rods provide the necessary shedding for the shuttle to pass through in the process of weaving. The shuttle contains the pirn on which the weft yarn is wound. The warp beam is primarily designed to provide the necessary tension while weaving and the cloth beam is used to reel the cloth woven. The shuttle travels to and fro and is thrown by hand from one end to the other. The warp-wise threads are called ends while the weft-wise threads are known as Picks. The Reeds used by weavers at Kanchipuram are manufactured out of bamboo sticks or stalks of cholam.

Manufacturing Process[17]

There are several stages in the process of manufacturing a Kanchipuram silk saree. Some of the most important stages will be studied here. The first stage is *purchase of raw silk* - Two types of silk sarees are produced at Kanchipuram, those which are woven out of pure silk without gold lace and the others, heavier and more lustrous called tissue sarees in which gold lace is used both for the body of the fabric as well as for the border. The raw silk is imported from Bangalore and the gold lace from Surat through local agents. The silk fabrics produced in Kanchipuram are woven out of pure mulberry silk yarn. Seventy two percent of the total production of mulberry silk yarn comes from Mysore State. Fifty percent of the raw silk produced in Mysore is consumed in Madras State. After obtaining the raw silk, twisting is done locally. Before raw silk is taken up for weaving, it has to undergo certain preparatory processes like *winding, twisting, degumming* and *dyeing.* The raw silk received by the weavers is dull in colour as it is normally coated over with a yellowish substance possessing the physical characteristics of gum. This coating has to be removed before silk is dyed. This process is known as degumming. The local name for this process is *USNA.* The yarn is dyed after *Usna*. Degumming and dyeing are also done simultaneously for certain colours.

Simultaneous Degumming and Dyeing

Two lbs. of raw silk are degummed and dyed at a time. The yarn is immersed in a cold bath containing coloured water. To obtain coloured water, coloured powder as per requirement is dissolved in two gallons of water. The quantity of powder depends upon the type of colour required and the exact nuances of shade and effect needed. After turning the yarn three or four times, it is taken out of the coloured bath, squeezed and inserted into 2 bamboo rods. The pots in which there is remnant of coloured water is then placed on the hearth, 5 gallons of water are poured into it and the temperature gradually raised. *Usna* soap weighing about 500 gms. is added to the solution. As soon as the temperature reaches 140^0 F., the raw silk held on the bamboo rods is immersed in this bath, turned three or four times, taken out and squeezed. When the water reaches boiling point, the yarn is once again immersed and turned once in 2 or 3 minutes. This immersion is of 15 minutes duration by which time the process of degumming and dyeing is completed. The yarn now appears wavy. It is then treated with acetic acid or lemon juice. This process is limited only to the following colours :

1. Brown
2. Nelson Blue
3. Grey
4. M.S. Blue
5. Manure
6. Chilli Red
7. Olive
8. Raw Coffee Seed Colour
9. Magenta

Degumming is to be done prior to dyeing for the following colours :

1. ICI Procion colour
2. Green
3. Black
4. Kanakambaram
5. Orange
6. Arakku
7. Rathi Blue
8. Ramar Green
9. Ananda
10. Violet

The weaver who receives the coloured warps proceeds with the following stages - *Dressing, Sizing, Piecing* and the next process locally known as *Aluppiduthal* i.e., mending of the broken ends. The preparations come to an end with this process and actual weaving operation commences with the following process :

Fixing the warp to the Loom

The yarn is divided on the loom into 18 segments. One end of it is fixed to the cloth beam and the other end to the warp beam. The distance between the cloth beam and the warp beam is 12 ft. For a normal 6 yards saree, the warp has to be stretched to this distance in order to weave 3 yards of the saree. After weaving this length, the warp has to be stretched once again to make a 6 yards saree. The length of the stretched warp should ensure tension while weaving for the free operation of the slay.

Preparation of the designs

The designs are prepared by alliances named Jungu or Adai made of bed-room lamp wicks and twine. Apart from the nine expert designers, there are several other designers also in Kanchipuram who prepare saree border designs on graph sheets and transfer the designs to the harness known as Adai. The weaver takes these design Adais to the loom in his house, gives the necessary cord connections while the gold threads on either side of the warp are drawn through the eyes of the Design healds. The next process is the joining of lace or gold thread which is a difficult process.

Next, is to prepare the Design Adai or Jungu, an outline saree border design is first drawn to scale on drawing paper and this is then traced on a sheet of graph paper. The necessary weaves are given to the designer and inked-in squares are marked by him on the gridded paper for the portions where figures come in. Now the design is ready for the harness or Adai preparation, a country style jacquard attachment whereby the various designs and patterns on the sarees are achieved. Now the loom is ready for weaving.

Weaving

This is the most important stage in the manufacturing of a Kanchipuram silk saree. The right end corner of the Jungu is pulled down and fixed to a nail 6" below its original position. The weaver presses down the right treadle of the loom to obtain the necessary shedding of the warp, throws the shuttle from the right hand side to the left and the pick is beaten. The right treadle is released and the left treadle pressed down to once again obtain the shedding and the weaver now throws the shuttle from the left to the right. Two picks are thus woven from one Jungu cord. The Jungu cord fixed to the nail is now released and the next cord is pulled down and attached to the nail. The shuttle is pushed from right to left and again in the reverse direction, the treadles being operated. In this way the cords are utilised to complete the design. Every time a new cord is pulled down and fixed to the nail, the weaver presses the right treadle and throws the shuttle from right to left.

Weaving of a double border saree

Most of the Kanchipuram sarees have contrast borders and borders on both sides ranging from 2" to 8" on each side. For this type of weaving, three shuttles are used. The weaver works the left side border and a boy weaves the right side with separate shuttles. This operation utilising three shuttles cover 5½ yards in a 6 yard saree and the Pallu, the wide border at the end of the saree, is produced conforming to the colour of the border. For this, another warp having the colour of the border is arranged over the existing warp and threads are drawn through the healds and the reed so that one thread of the old warp and one of this new warp are contained in each gap of the heald and four ends pass through each dent of the reed. The warp above is firmly held and woven closely for about 1" to 1½". After cutting out the warp ends the cloth is woven upto a length of 4" to 6". The threads of the earlier warp are cut out and the threads of the new warp retained and woven upto a length of ½ foot to complete the saree. The process of joining the Pallu of a different colour to the body of the saree is called "Petni". Extra wages are paid to this particular operation of blending together into a single piece-the body of the saree and the Pallu.

Cutting

Weaving is followed by two more stages viz., cutting and folding. After completing the pallu, the saree is carefully cut out of the loom with the help of a knife and the ends are neatly knotted into tassels. Then the saree is rolled on the cloth beam which is detached from the loom and the saree is unrolled from the beam and spread on a mat. The final stage is the folding.

Folding

The saree is first folded double from end to end and again folded double till its length is 27". The saree is again folded lengthwise so that its length is now 9", with the help of a smooth wooden rod the saree is folded width-wise twice from end to end so that the size becomes 9" x 11½". Care is taken to ensure that the Petni is always on the inside so that it is not soiled during inspection. The saree is then firmly pressed and knotted with a piece of twine and sent to the Co-operative Society. After inspection, a tag indicating the price and the size of the saree and bearing the name of the Co-operative Society is then attached to the saree and it is placed on the shelf for display. This is the glory of the Kanchipuram silk saree produced in South India. S.No. 26 - M.No. 77-XXV from Salar Jung Museum, show-case No.4 is a silk sari from Kanchipuram. It is a Black Sari with red border and has a check pattern in zari.

(C) Woollen

The weaving of wool has been practised extensively over North-Western India. People mostly use woollen cloth in the hills of Himachal Pradesh and Jammu and Kashmir and the cold regions of the North. Occasionally during marriages or festivals, the dresses differ. Villagers have a change in their dress according to seasons.

Fabrics made of wool, pashmina and goat hair have a special significance. In the cold regions of India particularly people living in mountaineous terrain use woollen articles commonly and atleast one person in every home spins. Spinning is very popular among men, women and children. They do it on a hand spindle known as *takli*. A weaver is commonly known as *Julaha*. It is difficult to trace and origin of their community. A few however, claim to be the descendents of the great poet Kabir who was a Julaha. Apart from those who are professional weavers, there are some who weave for their own domestic requirements. The art of weaving generally passes from generation to generation.[18]

Looms[19] :

Generally the weavers workshop is housed inside the room or in the verandah. The loom consists of several units such as cloth beam, warp beam, batten fitted with reed, healds with heddle horses or pulleys and harnesses, cords and strings, lams and paddles. There are atleast half a dozen shuttles, a dozen sticks, spools, bobbins, reed hooks and threading hooks, a scissors, an iron rod, spinning wheel and warping rack or peg board for preparing warp threads. The structure of the throw shuttle pit loom used by the villager is still the same old remote one. The loom is stretched horizontally on the ground and is supported generally by four posts, fixed deep in the ground in a rectangular form. The posts may be six in some cases. These are about 1½ feet above the ground. Beater and balance of heddles are attached to two or more wooden sticks suspended horizontally with a cord near the ceiling. Below the heddles there is one and a half feet deep pit in which four paddles are laid. The pit may be 1½ feet wide and 2½ feet long. The whole loom accessories are suspended from the ceiling and linked with strong thick cotton or woollen cords at various places to form the loom structure. Throw shuttle pit looms are very common in rural areas where weaving is commonly practised individually at home.

Tools and Equipment[20]

1. Tools used for preparing the yarn :
   i) Carders
   ii) Hand spindle
   iii) Wheel spindle
   iv) *Thernu* (creeping groove)
   v) *Taknosha* (small bowl)
2. Tools for preparing warp :
   i) Spool rack
   ii) Warping drum
   iii) Warping board
   iv) Warping mill
3. Other Accessories :
   i) Shuttle
   ii) Sticks
   iii) Bobbins
   iv) Bobbin winders
   v) Threading hook

Kashmir Shawls[21]

Of all the Indian woollen textiles none excel the beauty of colour texture and design of the richly patterned shawls of Kashmir. Shawl weaving is common in the North-Western part of India, but it is in Kashmir that it has reached its highest development. In *Ain-I-Akbari*, Abul Fazl enumerates about how the Emperor Akbar was fascinated by the shawls and the favour extended by him to the woollen industry of Kashmir. Much more has been written on these fascinating fabrics.

Manufacturing Process[22]

Raw Materials

Wool is the principal raw material used for weaving. The finest being *pashmina* - a derivative of *Pashim* which is goats' hair taken from the roots. It is conveyed from Tibet to Rudak on the backs of large sheep. It is brought to Leh - the chief town of Ladakh, where it is purchased by merchants of Kashmir.

Preparation of Pashmina yarn

Pashmina fibre is the wool of a goat known as 'chigu' goat. The fibre coat of this animal consists of two parts - a long straight coarse hair and a short fine undercoat. It is the undercoat which makes the fine soft material. Traders sell pashmina to villagers in impure form.

Sorting

Much attention is required to free the wool from the hair and the process is a tedious one. The soft fibre is separated. The sorter takes a small sliver of raw pashmina in his left hand and picks out thick hair one by one with his right hand. For sorting two kilograms, it would take working 6 to 8 hours every day a month.

Teasing and Spinning

The pure pashmina has greasy content which hinders in teasing and spinning. About 250 gms. of whitish clay is mixed thoroughly in it. This makes teasing easier. Teasing is carried on by pulling apart the fibres with hand. The process may be carried on a wooden comb. Each piece of teased wool is made into small slivers which are easily handled for spinning. Spinning is taken up either on hand spindles or wheel spindles. In this process, the cones are made smaller. Spinning of fleece or fibre in finer or coarse yarn basically depends on the quality of wool fibres. The yarn in counts of 60s is the finest and extremely thin in appearance. The fibre of pashmina being the finest, the thread spun from it would be as fine as of the 60 count. Besides, it is the skill of the experienced spinner who can spin the different qualities of wool finely. The pashmina fibre may be spun in yarn counts from 40s to 60s depending on the talented spinner.

Weaving Process - Preparation of the Warp

The first job of the weaver is to prepare warp and weft for the loom. Setting of warp threads is altogether different from those of the weft threads. The warping is an arrangement of long threads of equal lengths stretched over a loom kept parallel to the ground, this forms the structure of the material to be woven, and it forms the length of the cloth. This is the most complicated process. The warp is locally known as *Tana*. The yarn intended for warping is double and is cut into lengths of 3½ yards. Thread for the warp is usually made of a superior quality wool and is strongly twisted. Weavers prepare warp either by peg board warping process or stick warping methods. Before weaving the warp, yarn sheet has to pass through different operations such as tying of crosses, chaining or loose plaiting of the warp; spreading of the threads over the warp beam; drafting each warp end through the heddle eyes, passing of warp ends through the dents of the reed; and finally their tying up to the cloth roller in small groups. All these operations are completed particularly in fly shuttle looms when warps are laid on the looms. When the warp is fixed in the loom, the pattern drawer and the person who determines the proportion of yarn of different colours to be employed are consulted.

Preparation of Weft

The weft is known as *bana* in the weaver's terms. The threads of weft yarn are interlaced at right angles through the opening of the warp in an unbroken single thread. The thread is carried by shuttles. The weft yarn is single twist two ply thread.

The method of preparing weft, before it is put into operation is very simple. The weaver fills about half a dozen weft sticks at a time and keeps them close by.

Weaving

Two persons are employed in weaving a Kashmir shawl. One throws the shuttle from the edge as far as he can across the warp; it is then seized by the second weaver who throws it on the opposite end and then returns it. Weaving of the fabric goes on till the warp threads reach quite close to the healds. When the shawls are completed they are submitted to the cleaner who frees the shawl from discoloured hair or yarn and from ends or knots. The next stage is to fix the price for the shawl. Then the purchase takes the goods unwashed and when partly washed the dhobi brings the shawls to the merchant who examines them for any kind of imperfections. Then the completion of the washing is done in clear cold water and the coloured shawls are dried in shade while the white ones are bleached in the open air.

In the designing of patterns for Kashmir shawls, the treatment of form is one of the essential excellences, the designs which are either woven or embroidered. Sometimes the two processes are combined. Whether woven or embroidered it is almost always made of small pieces separately prepared and joined together so skillfully that the seams are scarcely visible. Assigning, choosing the colour scheme, and plotting the weave according to the needs of the design require a greater gift. The shawls exhibit an extensive variety of patterns and forms. The field is often densely packed with minute floral and foliar motifs, and occasionally figure subjects and architectural settings are also introduced. The colours are chosen to harmonize with the ground and with one another. Sometimes, the pattern is worked in such a manner that it appears the same on both the sides, this fabric is called a *dorukha*.

The innumerable shades of colours in the shawls of Kashmir embroidery support the theory that the riot of colours which go to the making, the gorgeous sunsets, the azure mountains, the sparkling lakes and the variegated flowers and birds, have left their indelible mark on the minds of the workers. The designs are evenly balanced. In designing a motif, the artist naturally selects from his own surroundings a subject which he can present compellingly and attractively, with an eye to colour and line. The main motifs in the designs are flowers, leaves, fruits and birds. Among birds, the most popular are the parrot, the magpie, the kingfisher, the woodpecker and the canary. Butterfly designs are also found, but flower and foliage are the dominant motifs. The popularly known shawl pattern is supposed to have been inspired by the cypress cone, almond or river loop in Kashmir and dominates most designs in some form or the other. The study includes twelve woollen textiles - Ten from the Salar Jung Museum and two from the State Museum, Hyderabad. S.No. 29 - M.No. 7107 from the collections of State Museum is a Tapestry with embroidery. The rest of the woollen pieces are shawls and mostly from Kashmir region. The S.Nos. 11, 12, 13, 14, 17, 19, 20, 22, 47 and 48 from Salar Jung Museum. Besides the Tapestry, mentioned above, the State Museum too consists of a woollen shawl, bearing M.No. 929 which is now in rags.

(D) Mixed Fabrics

Himroos of Aurangabad

The Himroo which forms the subject of this study is a fabric of intricate weave. The Himroo is fabric with cotton warp and silk or artificial silk, or rayon weft. The word 'Himroo' seems to be of Persian origin meaning 'proto type' or "of similar resemblance or features". This famous mixed fabric is being produced in the town of Aurangabad and the craft has survived till today inspite of keen competition from mill made cloth.[23]

Origin

Aurangabad is the home-town of Himroo. The origin of this fabric at Aurangabad is linked with the advent of Muslim rule in Southern India.[24] In the fourteenth century, many artisans came along with Mohammad Tughlak to Deogiri (Daultabad) and settled around this new capital. This craft was patronized by the nobles and courtiers of the Darbar as it was a fashion to wear this costly fabric at the time of attending the Darbar.[25] Later on, in about 1656 A.D. when Aurangzeb established Aurangabad as his Deccan Headquarters, these weavers shifted from Daulatabad to Aurangabad.[26] Since then, the name of Aurangabad came to be associated with the weaving of Himroo cloth. The Himroo cloth was very popular among the Nawabs and the craft had quite a flourishing period for two hundred years.[27] In the fourth decade of the present century, the Nizam's government took positive steps to help developing this craft and improving the facilities of marketing the finished goods. Orders were regularly placed from the Royal Palace for the Himroo fabrics.[28]

Technique of Production[29]

Most of the Himroo, weaving is carried out in Nawabpura locality situated to the North-East of Aurangabad town. Most of the residents here, in the past were Nawabs and Muslim nobles.

Generally, a part of the house is used as a workshop.

Tools and Implements

The tools and implements used are of the same design and make, as those in the use during the times of their forefathers. Almost all the tools and implements are manufactured through local carpenters. They comprise of the following :

1. Looms with all its parts including wooden frame, weaver's beam, pedals, reeds and heddles.
2. Throw shuttle *(Katla)*.
3. Wooden plough for holding the Jala threads in position *(Akoda)*.
4. 'V' shaped hook for lifting Jala threads *(Ambuda)*.

5. Warp bobbins.
6. Weft bobbins.
7. Winding charkha.
8. Warping

Description of the Loom[30]

The loom in use in Himroo weaving is the 'Throw shuttle loom'. The "Throw shuttle loom" is installed in front of a pit 3' x 3' x 3' at the rear end of which is fixed a wooden plank on the ground level for the weaver to sit on while operating the loom. Opposite to the weaver on the other side of the loom is fixed in the ground a crude wooden bench or stand about 2½' to 3' in height for the helper boy to sit.

The loom consists of a wooden frame having four vertical poles at each corner. The warper's beam on which the warp threads are wound is kept on a wooden frame at a height of about 6" from the ground, at a distance of about 6" on the other side of the loom. The warp threads are first passed through a net-work of threads, Jala, and then through four heddles held in position one after the other by strings, the other ends of which are tied to four separate bamboos. The bamboos holding the heddles in position are, at the other end, connected to four bamboo pedals or treadles at the feet of the weaver by means of separate strings. The pedals are in a slanting position and below each of them is a small pit, which, besides holding it in position, helps its operation when the weaver presses it with his foot. The particular heddle connected to the pedal is thus lifted up creating the required shed. At a distance of about two feet from the nearest heddle, on the weaver's side of the loom, is reed or *Hatta* as it is locally called, through which the warp threads are lastly passed. After passing through the reed, the warp threads are finally wound round the weaver's beam which is kept on a wooden frame at the feet of the weaver at a height of about 6" from the ground.

Raw Material

The major raw material required for the manufacture of Himroo cloth is yarn. It is cotton, staple and rayon (art-silk) and khadi and pure silk yarn. The other requirements is that of dyes. These raw materials and dyes are mainly purchased from Jalna and Bombay. Small purchases are made at Aurangabad only.

Manufacturing Process[31]

The various processes which are involved in the manufacture of a piece of Himroo cloth are:

Dyeing

The first stage is the preparation of the yarn for weaving. The threads that run lengthwise are called warp and those which run loose across are known as woof or weft yarn. The preparation of warp requires great care and caution. For dyeing the yarn, the dyeing-vat is kept on the furnace which is of the ordinary kitchen hearth type and fed on wood fuel. The dye-solution is heated to boiling point and the yarn is then immersed in it and kept there for half an hour, on the furnace. The yarn is then taken out of the solution, squeezed and oxidised in the air. When the required shade is obtained, the yarn is immersed in cold water, thoroughly washed, squeezed and dried.

After the yarn is completely dried, it is ready for further processing. The next stage is the winding of the yarn on bobbins. Next, when the required number of bobbins are ready, they are fixed on a wooden frame. The warp threads are then passed through the heddles, which are four in number for the production of Himroo cloth. After passing the warp thread through the heddles they are passed on through the reed, which is called 'denting'. For this, two persons are required. One to pick up the threads in succession and pass them through the reed and the other to pull them towards the weaver's beam with the help of a hook. They are then rolled over the beam before the weaving is started.

The next stage is to prepare the weft. The weft used is cotton and art-silk. This has to be dyed as explained in the first stage, mentioned above. The dried weft yarn is wound over the stalk piece with the help of the 'Winding Charkha'. The required number of stalks of cotton and art-silk yarn are prepared.

The last stage is 'weaving'. The weaving comprises interlacing the weft yarn with the warp yarns at right angle. Weaving consists of three stages :

1) Forming of sheds by lifting Jala doris and heddles;
2) Throwing shuttles across through these sheds;
3) Beating the filled in weft yarn into position with the reed.

Two persons are required in weaving of Himroo cloth, one to do the weaving and another, a helper boy, who sits on a bench above the loom, close to the Jala, to lift up the Jala threads as and when required, to obtain the shed on the warp sheet.

The process of weaving starts with the lifting of the required set of Jala threads with the help of *ambuda* alongwith the 'paga doris' (threads in horizontal position) which hold the loops through which the warp threads are passed. This results in the forming of cavities or boxes which are maintained through out the process. Simultaneously a shed is formed in the warp threads through which the weaver throws the shuttle of the coloured yarn of required tinge. When the required number of shuttles are thrown by the weaver, the *akoda* and *ambuda* are removed and the weaver beats the woven weft threads into position with the reed.

The weaver then presses one of the pedals at his feet thus lifting the heddle attacked thereby forming a different shed in the warp on the loom, through which he plies shuttle of black yarn for the required number of times depending upon the design of the cloth and beats and weft thread so woven into position with the help of the reed. The helper boy then lifts up another set of threads in the jala inserting *akoda*, as in the earlier case. Then follows the releasing of the jala by the helper boy and lifting of the heddle by the weaver and plying of black yarn shuttle which process is repeated in a given sequence depending upon the design till the complete length of the cloth is woven.

To manufacture a Himroo cloth with two-colour Mango Design of 30 yards x 30", on an average about 40 days are required.

The various designs in vogue at present are.[32]

i) Plain design - Plainlines, parallel line diagonal lines and lines intersecting each other.
ii) The Geometrical Designs - Circles, diamonds, hexagons, octagons, ovals and ellipses.
iii) Design from Nature - Fruits like pineapples, pome-granates, the almond and the mango.
iv) Designs of Flowers - Jasmine, the rose, the lily and the lotus.
v) Designs of Flowering Creepers.

vi) Designs of Birds and Animals - Elephants among the animals is the most popular one.

Religion also did not escape the artistic eye of the designer who often quoted verses from Quran were also woven in letters of gold, as aiso the portraits of ancient monarchs and the Hindu Gods and deities. The designs mentioned above are seen in the Himroos under study from the Museums of Hyderabad. In Salar Jung Museums' collections we come across these designs in textiles bearing the following S.Nos. 4, 40, 45, 68, 82, 84, S.No. 66 is a plain Himroo.

Articles produced in this craft are mostly shawls. The Himroo fabrics are also used for door and window curtains, tapestry, pillow-covers, skirts, dressing gowns, blouse pieces, ladies' money-purses and neck-ties. Himroo has still retained its original charm and is loved by discerning connoisseurs of textiles anywhere.[33]

References

1. Marg Publications - *Textiles & Embroideries,* Kamaladevi Chattopadhyaya (Editorial) p.56.
2. *The New Encyclopaedia Britannica Macropaedia,* 1981, Vol.18, 15th Edition Chicago, p.177.
3. Richardson, John. *Dictionary - Persian, Arabic and English,* p.849.
4. *Census of India,* 1961. Vol.XX, Part-VII-A. No.2, pp.7.
5. Brij Bhushan, Jamila. Op.Cit., 1958, p.65.
6. Ibid, p.65-69
7. George Walts & Percy Brown, Arts and Crafts of India, New Delhi, 1979, p.289.
8. Mehta J. Rustam. Op.Cit., p.97.
9. Richardson, John. Op.Cit., p.737.
10. Brij Bhushan, Jamila. Op.Cit., p.70.
11. Marg Publications. *"Indian Textiles in Historical Perspective",* John Irwin, p.4.
12. Sir George Watt. (Ed.). *Indian Art at Delhi,* pp. 290-292.
13. Brij Bhushan, Jamila. Op.Cit., 1958, p.70.
14. Census of India, 1961. Vol.IX, Part-VII-A, No.1, 'Silk Weaving of Kanchipuram', pp.1.
15. Ibid.
16. Ibid, pp.3.
17. Ibid, pp.7.
18. Census of India, Op.Cit., 1961. Vol.XX, p.8.
19. Ibid.
20. Ibid.
21. Ibid.
22. Ibid, pp.30.
23. Census of India, 1961, Himroos of Aurangabad, p.1.
24. Ibid.
25. Ibid.
26. Ibid.
27. Ibid.
28. Census of India, 1961. Vol.II, A.P. Part-VII-A, pp.39.
29. Census of India, 1961, Op.Cit., 1961, p.10.
30. Ibid.
31. Ibid, p.12.
32. Ibid, p.21-22.
33. Ibid.

CHAPTER - V

COLOUR AND DESIGN

The world of textiles cannot be visualised without endless shades of colours and infinite designs. It is on these bases that the textiles are classified because these factors indicate the characteristic features of a fabric and would indicate its provenance and period. The present chapter deals with the designs in relation with the colours found on the different textile objects in the Salar Jung Museum and State Museum, Hyderabad.

Colour

The use of dyes or colour in clothes was made since Harappan times. In the 6th and 7th century mural paintings in Ajanta caves are several colourful examples of beautifully patterned and striped clothes. However, the hues are limited in their varicty. After Ajanta, the show of colour on textiles nearly disappear till we reach the 12th century. When bolder dyeing and painting burst forth in Gujarati miniature paintings.[1] During mughal period mature patterns, ornate designs, brocaded glamour and bright flush of colours blossom forth matching the wealth and luxury of an aristocratic court.

In the west of India is the great colour belt stretching from Baluchistan through the deserts of Kathiawar and Rajasthan to Gujarat.[2] The people of this region showed their love for bright and big patches of flashing colours never seen in the past centuries. It looked a festival of colour in various combinations, the blazing crimsons with splashing blues, the burning vermillions with gorgeous yellows and the brilliant pinks with luscious greens.[3] As we go further south into the hills of Maharashtra, colours grow subtle and loose their startling brilliance till they quash themselves in the lush vegetation of the back waters of Malabar.[4] Here, white is the prime colour preferred by majority of the men and women.

Colour and design were the pivots on which fashion and styles revolved.[5] A superlative knowledge of colour chemistry and the use of indigenous dyes gives to the Indian woven and dyed clothes a quality of growth and enforcement. In the past, the dyes were made from juices of shrubs and herbs, fruits and flowers. The following are a few examples of Indian names identifying various shades of colour which provide substantial evidence of our earlier knowledge about the art of producing innumerable shades by mixing and treating different dyes in different proportions.[6]

Red and Yellow were mixed through different processes to obtain various shades of colour like *zafrani* (golden yellow), *campai* (saffron yellow), *narangi* (orange), *shabali* (light buff), and *gul-e-anar* (scarlet). Yellow and blue dyes mixed in different proportions produced *anguri* (grapes green), *pistai* (peagreen), *totai* (parrot green) and *tarbauzi* (bottle green). Blue and red combinations produced *sausani* (mauve), *kasni* (heliotrope) and *dilbahar* (lavender).

The extra-ordinary subtlety and comprehension of colour is manifest in the *Vishnudharmottara* where, white has five tones - Ivory white, Jasmine white, the white of an August moon, the white of August clouds when rain is spent and conch white.[7]

Designs

The chief designs and patterns studied in this chapter include :

I. The Kalamkaris

a) Kalamkaris of Kalahasti
b) Kalamkaris of Masulipatnam

II. Embroideries

a) Kasida works of Kashmir
b) Phulkari of Punjab
c) Brocades

A study of the origin and development of printed textiles is rendered extremely difficult as there are no specimens extant of early printed textiles in our country. The earliest specimen of Indian resist-dyed cloth dates back to the 8th century.[8] According to Saraswati, the field of Indian Textiles is a very extensive one and for a better understanding of this complex subject, it is desirable to make some classifications at the outset. Broadly, Indian textiles may be divided into two groups - plain and patterned. The patterned ones may be further classified according to the way in which the patterns are produced. These can be studied under two main heads :

1. Those textiles in which artistic treatment is given subsequent to the weaving.
2. Those in which artistic treatment is given while they are on the loom. The first include all textiles which issue plain from the loom and receive their decoration and final treatment at the hands of the dyer, the printer or the embroiderer. The second refers to those materials which the decoration is woven in to the fabric, either through the manipulation of the loom or as in tapestries by means of an additional shuttle. The decoration or designing thus forms an integral part of the process of manufacture.

Perhaps the earliest reference to the printed fabrics is found in the word 'Chitranta' in the *Apastambha Srauta Sutra* (XIX, 20)[9]. In both the Epics there are references to printed cloth. It is said that dyeing of textiles was practised from Vedic times. The patterns used for printing textiles can be classified according to the region in which they are manufactured. The designs generally used in the north are quite distinct from those current in the south, but the beauty of pattern and colour is remarkable every where in the country.[10]

By printed textiles is meant all fabrics on which a pattern is produced subsequent to the weaving of the cloth, by the application of dye-stuff or pigment to the surface of the fabric. This can be done in many ways.[11]

a) By the direct or application process.
b) By the resist or indigo process.

c) By the mordant, madder, alizirine or modern discharge process.
d) Tinsel printing.

By the direct or application process which implies the use of the woollen block or silk screen directly on the fabric known as the block printing and screen printing process.

Second method is by the resist or indigo process. This implies covering nor impregnating certain portion of the cloth which are intended to be kept in the background colour, with wax, clay, gum, resin or other resist, so that when the cloth is subsequently dyed, the colour does not penetrate the portion which have been previously impregnated with the resist. This produces the desired pattern. Block-printing may be subsequently carried out after the cloth, which have retained their original colour. The resist substance may be applied by brush or kalam, by block or by hand.

In the mordant or alizirine process, the cloth is prepared with various mordants prior to the use of the dye. When the cloth is then immersed in a dye bath, a chemical reaction of the dye on the mordant produces different colours on the cloth, only those portions which have been prepared take the dye. Various shades are produced by various variable use of the mordant. The colours that emerge have great depth and brilliance. The mordant or the dye can be applied both by brush or by block. The cloth is dyed in the desired background colour in the modern discharge process. The pattern is then printed on with chemicals, which results after further treatment, in the removal of the background colour from those portions where chemicals have been so applied. The discharged parts of the design can then be further processed.

Application of a thick pigment which is made by mixing a yellow powdered colour with castor oil and then heating the mixture, to the fabric can produce patterns which appear to be encrusted on the fabric. When gold colour is added in the pigment, it is known as Tinsel printing. Salar Jung Museum S.No. 23 - M.No. 62-18.

The techniques, designs and patterns of textiles are very distinctive. The styles were determined by geographical factors and cultural influences brought in by waves of migratory tribes which has greatly influenced the development of different styles of textile weaves. Two main trends seem to have been established in the printing tradition, arising the urge in man to decorate the garments he wore and based on a common technique. In the present study we encounter printed textiles mostly in the show case No.12 of the Salar Jung Museum. The earliest of them is dated to the 17th century S.No.98 - M.No. 63-85 a cotton Pichchwai from Rajasthan.

Lester Griswold[12] opined that an interpretation of art as applied to crafts refers to design as expressed in a material having dimensions of form and proportion as well as qualities of colour and texture. The craftsman must first visualise the design and within the limitations or possibilities of the material, embody in a piece of craftwork the honest expression of his ideas, developed in accordance with the specific purpose or function of the finished work. This requires imaginative understanding of the material and the technique of design, as well as the mastery of the skills and procedures through which his creative idea may be expressed.

The mosaic or inlay tradition patronized by the moghuls were the sophisticated and painted fabrics that were created under their patronage. The most famous centres for the mosaic or inlay tradition were Masulipatnam, Kalahasti and Palakollu in Andhra Pradesh. The cloths of these centres in South were known as "KALAMKARI"[13] S.Nos. 27, 96, 101, 102, 110, 112, 116, 119,

120 from Salar Jung Museum are from Andhra Pradesh. The Kalamkari pieces from State Museum bearing S.Nos. 46 - M.No. 1050-51; S.No. 74 - M.No. 6868-69; S.No. 34 - M.No. 78-26; S.No. 59 - M.No. 80-21; S.No. 73 - M.No. 6791; etc.

I. KALAMKARI TEXTILES

Early Kalamkaris with human figures consisted only of incidental and unreleated figure groups which the cotton painted incorporated as subordinate elements in designs of his own decorative conception.[14] The design of one Kalamkari piece referred to by John Irwin[15] is composed of six pillared compartments surmounted by *makara* heads, each framing a group of figures in South Indian dress. At the top, there is a row of *mandapas* and *gopuras* of Hindu temple pavilions in conventional South Indian style of late 16th century, interspersed with coconut and other trees, monkeys and birds. One of the riches in the architecture shows Ganesa. Perhaps the design represents the royal donor of some temple along with his queens and was intended for some descendent of the Vijayanagara royal family.

A Kalamkari artist, at work would know that drawing quickly a human figure with melted at wax using a bamboo pen require real control over form and line. It has to be done in a single stroke and working on coarse cloth is not as easy a task as working on art paper. It requires generations of hard work and dedication to gain real expertise, the existence of the tradition can be taken back to 1542 A.D. when the Lepakshi temple murals were executed.[16] The detailed treatment of the textile designs of the garments worn by the characters of the Lepakshi mural can be matched only by Kalamkari hanging. This heightened awareness of fabric designing turning almost into an obsession could come naturally only to those who were basically engaged in textile printing and were incidentally employed to paint murals. The sway of the garments worn by the figures in the murals support the above opinion. The colours used, the sinuous lines and the quick and tender strokes all proclaim that it was a temple hanging painter, who executed the murals at Lepakshi.[17] The artists of Lepakshi were familiar with Saivite and Vaishnavite religious themes and composed panels for narrating stories of the *Puranas*. The Kalamkaris for diverse usage were made in famous centres such as Masulipatnam, Palakollu, Kalahasti and Tadpatri. The craftsmen at all these centres specialised in illustrating stories from the *Puranic* legends and from the *Ramayana* and *Mahabharata*. The art form is still a living one at Kalahasti and Masulipatnam.

a) Kalamkari Temple Cloth Painting of Kalahasti

Kalahasti, situated on the bank of river Swarnamukhi is a pilgrim centre where a very imposing and fine temple devoted to Lord Kalahasteswara is located. In this place of religious importance arose the industry of Kalamkari temple cloth painting.[18] The imbibed ritual of the Hindu Temple where the pleasure of gods was evoked, especially in the shrines of South India, made constant demand for temple hangings. And Kalahasti, where the figures of gods were painted, as well as the myths and legends described, has continued to hypnotise the folks. These pictures unravel the mysteries of the faith of the oral culture.[19] Kalahasti and its surroundings were under the control of zamindars. The religious importance of the place and the patronage of the zamindars must have undoubtedly proved propitious for the development of the industry here. The tradition of making temple hangings still continues.[20]

There is no information about how and when the industry originated. The local people believe that perhaps the Kalamkari printers of Masulipatnam, who has specialised in Kalamkari printing for centuries might have passed on their knowledge to the Kalahasti workmen who developed their own designs to suit the local demand and specialised in temple cloth printing. The Kalahasti temple cloth painting and printing is done entirely by Kalamkari process, i.e., with the help of a Kalam or Pen.[21] But the technique differs somewhat from the well-known Kalamkari printing of Masulipatnam. In the case of Kalahasti product, the designs which consist of mythological human figures, flowers, border designs etc., are all drawn free hand with a Kalam. The designs of the temple cloths of Kalahasti are wholly dependent upon individual skill of both the hand and the imagination. They can be drawn only by the expert artist and this requires considerable patience and great competency in draughtsmanship. The Kalahasti craftsman specialises only in the designs needed for temple cloths which consist of panels depicting the stories from the epics. No wax processing is involved in the Kalahasti technique.[22]

It is somewhat surprising that there is no standard book of designs or scenes from which the artist-craftsman can copy out his panels.[23] The reproduction of theme seems to be based purely on tradition. Though there is no standardisation, there is an amazing similarity in the colours, the purely decorative designs, the spatial divisions of the compositions and the forms, postures and expressions of the figures. These figures have a graphic uniqueness of their own. The Kings, Rishis, Gods, Goddesses, Rakshasas, Demons etc., are full of an alive and plastic grace and dignity without any formal art school education, the artist produces these figures free-hand. The pupil learns the rudiments of designs from his master and also from the greatest teacher of all the ancient temple cloths themselves. Even the wording of the titles that are painted with the Kalam containing the black dye along the borders of the design to interpret each scene of a panel, have no standardisation. The artist explains briefly and clearly what each scene represents.

As has already been pointed out, Kalahasti Kalamkari work specialises in producing temple cloths used as canopies over the idols during festival celebrations or as panels to hang on the walls to provide a background for religious functions. The themes adopted for the designs are from the Epics and the Puranas. The following are some of them:[24]

1. Dhruva Vijayam
2. Daksha Yajnam - Salar Jung Museum S.No. 116, M.No. 62-51.
3. Dasavataram
4. Sitarama Kalyanam, - Salar Jung Museum S.No. 120, M.No. 63-55.
5. Sampoorna Ramayanam - Salar Jung Museum S.No. 110, M.No. 216-CSI.
6. Mahabharata Virataparvam - Salar Jung Museum S.No. 111, M.No. 1-XLII.
7. Venkateswara Charitam.

The panels usually have attractive and decorative borders within which the scenes are contained. The court scenes and marriage pandals in particular are embellished with beautiful line drawings in the borders.[25]

A close look at the murals on the Ranga Mandapa of Lepakshi temple reveals certain interesting characteristics of the paintings.[26] To begin with the first impact which these murals make is that of a back-drop which is meant to provide a setting to the stage of some drama - a purpose not very different from that of a temple hanging.

b) Kalamkari Cloth Printing of Masulipatnam

The "Chintz" and "Calicos" of Masulipatnam had received world-wide recognition and occupied a pride of place amongst the Indian textile products from the earliest times.[27] It is obvious that Masulipatnam port was one of the well-known ports of the ancient sea routes of the world. It is believed that the hand printed cloth of Masulipatnam was popular with the Greeks even before Christ. Thus the calico printing and dyeing industry of Masulipatnam held an undaunted sway till about the middle of the 18th century. The earliest known piece extant of a Kalamkari work can be dated to the beginning of the eighteenth century. The portuguese attempted to monopolise the sea-trade with India in the 15th century and the goods include Kalamkari furnishings with floral and geometrical designs which were imported by them in the East Indians in exchange of spices.[28]

Describing the dyeing Industry of Southern India, the Imperial Gazetteer writes.[29] "In Masulipatnam and elsewhere in Southern India, admirable chintzes have for many centuries been turned out, which are really handprinted textiles, so perfectly coloured that it is sometimes difficult to distinguish them from the finest embroidery".

The technique of the Kalamkari painting of Masulipatnam consists of the application of the colours to a cloth by means of a pen or Kalam on certain portions and certain other portions rendered impervious to the colour by the application of molten bee wax.[30] The Kalamkari specimens of Masulipatnam are firstly block printed and then the colours are painted with a Kalam. The high quality of Masulipatnam painting is ascribed to the use of "cherry" plant which is said to have grown wild, in the area over flown with spring tides at the mouth of the "Krishna Delta" or was it the effect of broken or rotten shells in the sandy soil.[31] The Kalamkari industry of Masulipatnam claims that the dyes were all of pure vegetable origin which are said to give strength to the cloth unlike the chemical dyes which adversely affect the texture of the cloth. Thus the calico printing and dyeing industry of Masulipatnam held an undaunted sway till about the middle of the 18th century.[32]

The printed cottons of Masulipatnam consisted of canopies, screen cloths, prayer cloths etc.[33]

The Masulipatnam cloth dyers produced various types of printed material[34] - canopies with special mythological designs for the Hindus, the prayer carpets for the Mohammadens with their typical Middle Eastern designs, the tent lining cloth which was a favourite of the Persian rulers, the chintz i.e., small printed designs on cloth by the yards of special designs to suit the tastes of the Westerners, table cloths and curtain cloths printed in most attractive colours and designs, sarees and dhotis to meet the needs of the local consumer. The demand for these textiles was universal and the craftsmen excelled in their art to satisfy the tastes of one and all.

The Salar Jung Museum and State Museum possess beautiful Kalamkari Textiles belonging to different places and different periods. The Kalamkaris on view represent mainly the episodes from Epics, the Ramayana and the Mahabharatha. From Salar Jung Museum collections S.No. 110 - M.No. 216-CSI; S.No. 111 - M.No. 1-XLII; S.No. 119 - M.No. 215-CSI; S.No. 120 - M.No. 63-55;

Kalamkari's from State Museum with scenes from the Epics - S.No. 46 - M.No. 1050-51; S.No. 34 - M.No. 78-26; S.No. 47 - M.No. 2353; S.No. 51 - M.No. 87-44; S.No. 55 - M.No. 5611.

II. EMBROIDERY

Embroidery or the decoration of woven fabrics with coloured threads by means of a needle is probably one of the oldest arts of the world. In India it dates from the remotest period of history. Embroidered garments and needles are mentioned in Vedic texts and the art of embroidery flourishes in all parts of India down to this day.

Embroidery is acknowledged as of oriental origin. India is said to be one of its original homes. The reference to embroidery in the Vedas and later in the Epics prove their antiquity. The reference to *pesas* in Vedic literature is understood as connoting embroidered garments. The Mohenjodaro excavations revealed bronze needles used for embroidery dating back to c.2300-1500 B.C. The figurines found at the Indus Valley excavations site are seen with embroidered drapery. Amongst the old Buddhist stupas and sculptures, the figurines are found with embroidered wrappings. So also the later Kushan sculptures. Embroideries can also be seen in the garments depicted in the Ajanta frescoes. With the impact of the Persian embroidery in the Mughal days, some of the early styles were modified and these have continued to the present time. This blend was carefully brought about by the Moghul rulers, initiated during Akbar's reign, by running big embroidery workshops in which the two styles Indian as well as Persian intermingled to produce a new one. These embroideries were being exported outside India. Foreign visitors to India in their chronicles too referred to embroidered garments. The Sanskrit dramas, especially of Kalidasa, describe embroidered dresses worn by various characters.[35]

Embroidery is a process carried out only after the cloth leaves the loom. The field that embroidery occupies in India is most extensive and ranges from the simplest herring-bone patterns of the aborigines to the elaborate figure compositions of chamba and the intricate chikan work of Lucknow.[36]

Though certain basic stitches may be common in all embroidery, each region has developed distinct characteristics of its own because embroidery also reflects the local tradition, culture and physical environments. It is this which has given so many different faces to Indian embroidery. Each is rooted in the original folk culture from which each has evolved, and each has its predominant designs, colour combinations and techniques.[37]

A very cheap type of cotton or calico often forms the background for the most elaborate and expensive embroidery. The thread employed in embroidery is usually of wool or silk. Gold or silver threads are also widely used. The stitches generally used in Indian embroidery are satin, darn, stem and chain. Many variations of these four principal forms of stitches exist in India. The chief designs and patterns studied comprise of the following :

a. Kasida embroidery of Kashmir.
b. Phulkari of Punjab.
c. Brocades of Benaras, etc.

A. Kasida Embroidery of Kashmir

Origin

Perhaps the most famous of them all is the Kashmir embroidery. It is one of the most striking in India, depending for its beauty not so much on the intricacy of the stitches as on vivid colours tastefully blended. The art is said to have been introduced there in the 15th century by Zain-ul-Abdin Shah who brought in Persian craftsmen to teach it to its natives.[38] One peculiar feature of its workers is the fact that it is done almost entirely by men, unlike elsewhere where it is almost wholly done by women.[39] The embroideries of this region seem so overwhelmed by nature's riotous beauty that they are caught up in its alluring embrace. The floral motifs, with their inexhaustible display of colours, the majestic mountains, the shimmering lakes, the variegated birds and the luscious fruits all find a place in the Kashmir embroidery which is executed with meticulous care.[40] Kasida flourished principally in Srinagar and some of the surrounding towns.

Technique

Kasida work is variously classified, and special names are given to different types. *Kashidan* in Persian, literally means "to draw", and in India Kashida refers to most embroideries done with silk thread using the basic stitches of Kashida - running, satin, stem, chain and sometimes darning or herring bone stitches.[41] Kashmir Kashida made on both silk and wool uses basic Kashida stitches. One outstanding feature of this embroidery is the fact that it is done with single thread giving a flat, formalised appearance to the design, while the satin stitch is adopted to cover large surfaces without pressurising the cloth. The finest kasida, particularly, on shawls and saris, has no wrong side. The same fineness is displayed on both sides so as to make the wrong side indistinguishable from the right, and the Kashmir workman has made himself an adept at this art.

Varieties

The Kashmir embroiderer has given special names to different types such as *rafugari, zalak dozi, vata-chikan, doria* and *talaikar*.[42] When the stitch is on both sides it is known as *Dorukha*. Of these, rafugari is worked in the darning stitch and done on scarves and rare shawls and involving a great deal of labour and commanding high price. The background material used is either silk or wool.

B. Phulkari of Punjab

Origin

Flower-work is a traditional craft of Punjab. *Phulkari* means 'Flowering work' and might therefore be applied to any embroidery. The origin of phulkari is associated with the brave and industrious Jats who occupy the districts of south-east Punjab and parts of the adjoining areas of the United Provinces. But the most important centre of Phulkari is Rohtak. The Jats appear to have carried the art of phulkari embroidery with them wherever they went. Traces of this kind of art are also found in Rajasthan which includes Jats among its population. It is interesting to find that some of the designs being similar to Kasuti designs of the Karnatak. It is quite possible that some migratory tribes might have carried the designs to and fro.[43]

Technique

Phulkari work is laborious and slow. There are different formulae for the various patterns which are said to be handed from mother to daughter and from friend to friend. This is worked in silk floss on cloth which is especially woven for the purpose. The base of phulkari embroidery is coarse khaddar-like cloth, of red or blue colour and the motifs of the design are floral, as the name itself implies.[44] The design is worked on the reverse side of the cloth with strands of untwisted silk. The base is fully covered by the embroidery in the best phulkari work, so that it becomes difficult to distinguish the fabric from the embroidery. The base is so fully covered, that the embroidery itself now becomes the cloth and the merger is complete. The work is usually done on oblong pieces of material about 2½ yards long and 1¾ yards wide.[45]

Varieties

There are three main types of phulkari. The first being the true phulkari where the pattern is diapered at intervals over the cloth.[46]

The second is called *bagh* or 'garden' where the whole surface is decorated with a connected pattern. The 'bagh' has several names, e.g., Shalimar Bagh, Kakri Bagh, Chand Bagh, Mircha Bagh, Dhunia Bagh etc., depending on the motif used in the work.[47] The remarkable fact is that with the skillful manipulation of the darning stitch so many varieties of complicated designs are created, with a total effect of floral magnificence.

The third type is known as the *chobe*, and here the edges alone are embroidered while the centre is left plain.[48]

Yellow, white, green and red are the four colours invariably preferred in selecting silk floss for phulkari work, although the shades of any particular colour used are not always the same. When other colours such as blue or purple, introduced into phulkari work, it is sure that the article is not genuine. The beauty and workmanship are the chief characteristics of genuine phulkari work which can never be rivalled by the cheap imitations put on the market. The textile worker has copied some of the phulkari designs for making his borders. The width of such borders is however limited to a few inches only.[49] While dealing with the phulkari work of the Punjab, it is necessary to make a passing reference to the embroidery of the Middle East, and of Baluchistan, which discloses the use of the darning stitch, but the way in which this type of stitch has been developed to produce exquisite designs has put the work of Punjab in a class by itself.[50]

The making of 'Phulkari' is a matter of great pride to the Jats of Punjab. The 'phulkaris' are presented to the daughter at the time of marriage. One piece is worn by the girl at the time of the marriage ceremony. Other pieces are used for bed covers, quills, etc.[51]

The imitations put in the market have brought about deterioration in the art of the phulkari embroidery. Economic causes have contributed to the deterioration of the art, and the tendency has been to sacrifice quality to quantity.[52]

Speaking of phulkari work, no one can omit to mention the great service rendered to Indian Art and Industry by Mrs. F.A. Steele by her splendid article on "Phulkari work in the Punjab". She shows her keen desire that the beauty of Phulkari should be zealously preserved as an integral part of the romance in the life of the Jatni maiden.[53]

Salar Jung Museum displays excellent Phulkari Work. S.No. 8 - M.No. 21/XL, S.No. 41 - M.No. 65-XLII, S.No. 42 - M.No. 1-XXII, S.No. 44 - M.No. 65-XLII. S.No. 56 - M.No. 5613, and S.No. 57 - M.No. 6490, are Phulkari's from State Museum, Hyderabad.

C. Brocades

Origin

The term 'brocade' is sometimes made to embrace all flowered or patterned silks in which the patterns are woven, not printed. The root of the word 'brocade' is identical with that in 'broach' and means "to stab" or "transfix".[54] Brocade fabrics of India have earned a great reputation for their craftsmanship and grandeur. The silk brocades of Benaras, Ahmedabad and Surat were well-known in the seventeenth century while Benaras continues to be a centre of production for silk brocades, Ahmedabad and Surat have practically nothing left to show today. Kinkhobs or brocades worked out in gold or silver thread occupy a unique position in the wide range of Indian Textiles.[55] Among the different types of embroidery known to exist in India gold and silver embroidery has perhaps, the most ancient and interesting history. It is the oldest known embroidery and the most widespread. Reference to gold fabric in India is found in the *Yajurveda*, the *Satapatha Brahmana* and in the two great epics of India. The kinkhob, or gold and silver brocade industry of India is famous and has been referred to in the *Jatakas*.[56] Both 'cloth of gold' and kinkhob are mentioned in the Vedas. Megasthenes,[57] speaking of the costumes of the princes of India, remarks that their robes were worked in pure gold. The kinkhobs were originally woven of pure gold and that silk was added both to give the body the texture and afford a means of colour illumination.

The gold and silver thread industry of India exists in several cities and towns which are important as trading centres or as places of historical or political significance. These include Delhi, Bhopal, Lucknow, Benaras, Murshidabad, Ahmedabad, Surat, Bombay, Aurangabad, Hyderabad (Deccan) and Madras. Kinkhobs are mainly produced in Benaras, Ahmedabad and Surat.[58] Coming to the gold and silver embroidery proper, known as *Karchob*, it may be classified into two main categories. *Zardozi* is the name given to the heavier and more elaborate variety in which stitches are very close to each other. The less elaborate, or lighter, embroidery on finer fabrics is called *Kamdani*.[59]

Technique

For making gold and silver thread called *Kalabattoo* the following method is used:[60] For gold thread a piece of silver about the length and thickness of a man's finger is gilded at least 3 times with the purest gold, all alloy being previously most carefully discharged from the silver. This piece of guilt wire is beaten out to the size of a stoutwire and is then drawn through successive holes in a steel plate until the wire, literally, as fine as hair. It is then flattened in an extremely delicate and skillful manner. This is all done with such skill that it seems as though a highly sensitive machine had been working on the wire.

The method of drawing the wire upon silk thread is equally ingenious. A very slightly twisted silk is rolled upon a winder, the end passing over a polished steel hook fixed to a beam. From it, is suspended a spindle with a long thin bamboo shank weighted to keep it steady.

A sharp turn is given to the shank by the workman upon his thigh, to set it spinning rapidly. The gold wire wound on a reel as it passes the workman, is applied to the bottom of the silk thread near the spindle and allowed to twist itself upwards upon the thread as high as the workman can conveniently reach. The dexterity and near perfection with which this is manipulated is incredible. The uniform thickness, flexibility, softness and ductility are remarkable.[61] The flattened wire or badla is used for making 'Kamdani' work. The workmen who make this thread are called *batwaiya* or *kalabattoo - nakad*. The weaver of the cloth with *kalabattoo* is called *tashbaff*.[62]

Varieties and Uses

Gold and Silver embroidery is known as *Karchob*. (S.No. 51 - M.No. 68-XXIV; S.No. 55 - M.No. 6-XLIX). The zardozi, the heavier and more elaborate is used for masnads, floor coverings, bed covers, cushions, animal trappings, canopies and shoes. The ground work for these heavy embroideries is usually velvet, satin or heavy silks. These materials were once, also used on sheaths and handle covers for swords. Also in tents and a saddle-cloth. Kamdani is the lighter embroidery done on lighter material like wearing apparel, caps, scarves and veils.[63]

The other varieties are *mina*, The *kataoki beli*, The *hazara buti* etc. superb and very varied work is done also on leather, felt and velvet, usually used on animals, carts, footwear, handbags, chogas and overcoats.[64]

Silk brocade weaving has gained ground in the South. The situation is similar in cotton brocade weaving, while silk and cotton fabrics of chanderi silk continue to be woven. The cotton jamdani fabrics of Tanda are now almost non-existent, while the production of other types of brocaded cotton fabrics is growing in Venkatagiri as well as in other southern centres. The main centres in Andhra Pradesh are :

1. Venkatagiri 2. Dharmavaram 3. Pochampalli 4. Gadwal 5. Uppala and 6. Kothapalli.

The Salar Jung and State Museums possess Textiles with excellent embroidery work chiefly from Benaras and the regions around. They are : S.No. 24 - M.No. 62-38-1; S.No. 25 - M.No. 67-XXV; S.No. 43 - M.No. 22-XVI; S.No. 46 - M.No. 78-XXIV; S.No. 51 - M.No. 68-XXIV; S.No. 52 - M.No. 2-XXIV; S.No. 55 - M.No. 6-XLIX; S.No. 56 - M.No. 367-XLIX; S.No. 57 - M.No. 56-XXIV from Salar Jung Museum and from State Museum S.No. 29 - M.No. 7107; S.No. 28 - M.No. 8755 are from Kashmir.

References

1. Biswas, A. *Op.Cit.,* 1985, p.112.
2. Chattopadhyay, Kamaladevi (Ed.). *Op.Cit.,* p.7.
3. Biswas, A. *Op.Cit.,* 1985, p.112.
4. Chattopadhyay, Kamaladevi (Ed.). *Op.Cit.,* p.7.
5. Biswas, A. *Op.Cit.,* 1985, p.112.
6. Ibid.

7. Marg Publications - *Op.Cit.,* p.6.
8. Saraswati, S.K. *Op.Cit.,* p.3.
9. Brij Bhushan, Jamila - *Op.Cit.,* 1958, p.25.
10. Saraswati, S.K. *Op.Cit.,* 1961, p.3.
11. Marg Publications - *Homage to Kalamkari - "Gaiety in Colour and Form"* by Pupul Jayakar, p.23,
12. Griswold Lester - *Handicraft - Simplified procedure and projects,* p.7
13. Hadway, W.S. *Cotton Painting and Printing in Madras Presidency,* 1917, p.20.
14. Irwin, John - "Golconda Cotton Paintings of the Early 17th Century". *Lalit Kala No.5,* 1959, p.29.
15. Ibid.
16. Varma, D.N. *Itihas Vol.III - No.1,* 1980, "The Kalamkaris in the Temples of A.P." p.142.
17. Ibid.
18. Census of India, 1961, Vol.II *Op.Cit.,* p.39.
19. Marg Publications - Homage to Kalamkari, *Op.Cit.,* p.11.
20. Census of India, 1961, *Op.Cit.,* p.39.
21. Ibid., p.40.
22. Census of India, 1961, p.41.
23. Ibid., p.46.
24. Ibid, p.46.
25. Ibid.
26. Varma, D.N. *Op.Cit.,* 1980, p.148.
27. Census of India, 1961, p.53-54.
28. Mittal, Jagadish - Correlation and Assimilation between the Arts and Crafts of India and the Western World. Salar Jung Museum, *Bi-annual Research Journal* Vol.IX-X, 1976-77, p.41.
29. *The Imperial Gazetteer of India,* 1908, Vol.III, p.177.
30. Ibid.
31. Irwin, John - *Op.Cit.,* 1959, pp.18-19.
32. The Imperial Gazetter of India, 1908, Vol.III, p.64.
33. The Imperial Gazetter of India, *Op.Cit.,* 1908, p.64.
34. Census of India, 1961, *Op.Cit.,* p.53-54.
35. Chattopadhyay, Kamaladevi (Ed.). *Op.Cit.,* p.5.
36. Saraswati, S.K. *Op.Cit.,* 1961.
37. Chattopadhyay, Kamaladevi (Ed.). *Op.Cit.,* p.5.
38. Brij Bhushan, Jamila - *Op.Cit.,* 1958, p.51.
39. Saraswati, S.K. *Op.Cit.,* 1961.
40. Chattopadhyay, Kamaladevi (Ed.). *Op.Cit.,* p.5.
41. Brij Bhushan, Jamila - *Op.Cit.,* 1958, p.50.
42. Dongerkery S. Kamala - *Op.Cit.,* 1951, p.18.
43. Ibid, p.45.
44. Ibid, p.26.
45. Brij Bhushan, Jamila - *Op.Cit.,* 1958.
46. Saraswati, S.K. *Op.Cit.,* 1961.
47. Brij Bhushan, Jamila - *Op.Cit.,* 1958, p.52.
48. Saraswati, S.K. *Op.Cit.*
49. Dongerkery S. Kamala - *Op.Cit.,* 1951, p.26-27.
50. Ibid.
51. Brij Bhushan, Jamila - *Op.Cit.,* 1958, p.52.
52. Dongerkery S. Kamala - *Op.Cit.,* 1951, p.28.

53. Ibid, p.27.
54. George Watts & Percy Brown (Eds.) *Op.Cit.,* p.319.
55. Saraswati, S.K. *Op.Cit.*
56. Dongerkery S. Kamala - *Op.Cit.,* 1951, p.46-47.
57. George Watts & Percy Brown (Eds.) *Op.Cit.,* p.320.
58. Dongerkery S. Kamala - *Op.Cit.,* 1951, p.47-48.
59. Ibid., p.48.
60. Brij Bhushan, Jamila - *Op.Cit.,* 1958, p.54.
61. Chattopadhyay, Kamaladevi (Ed.). *Op.Cit.,* p.10.
62. Brij Bhushan, Jamila - *Op.Cit.,* 1958, p.54.
63. Chattopadhyay, Kamaladevi (Ed.). *Op.Cit.,*
64. Ibid.

CHAPTER - VI

UTILITY

The chapter deals with, the utility of various fabrics and textiles dealt with in the present study. The textiles are classified into :

(A) Sewn Garments and (B) Unsewn Cloth (C) Furnishing Materials (D) Mixed Fabrics

A. SEWN GARMENTS

Choga

This is a long loose robe extending upto the ankles with an open in the front. It was generally worn by men of upper class. (S.No. 1 - M.No. 62-11; S.No. 3 - M.No. 62-31; S.No. 40 - M.No. 62-26; S.No. 45 - M.No. 62-31-4; S.No. 106 - M.No. 62-50; etc. from Salar Jung Museum and S.No. 18 - M.No. 6502; S.No. 19 - M.No. 6503; from State Museum.

Chowbaghla

This is also a type of loose robe fitting having four cuts to give a shape (S.No. 7 - M.No. 84-XXIV from Salar Jung Museum).

Sherwani

This was called as *'Achkan'* when it was first designed. The Sherwani proper is used as an article of attire, an upper garment, of Muslim men which came into being during the latter part of the Muslim period. This long coat reaches slightly below the knees, closing down the front. (S.No. 5 - M.No. 62-84 from Salar Jung Museum and S.No. 54 - M.No. 1561 from State Museum).

Angarkha

It is a tunic, reaching almost to the knees. The men wore a dhoti and an '*Angarkha*' and the waist was bound by a scarf known as the 'Patkha' or '*Kamarbandh*'. The angarkha, was generally, pure white and a light garment made of muslin, worn during summer. It was also made of silk depending on the rank of the wearer. The Mughals wore the *angarkhas* before the invention of the '*Sherwani*'. (S.No. 105 - M.No. 65-XXIV; S.No. 107 - M.No. 83-XXIV from Salar Jung Museum).

Kurta

Tunic tight to the waist with a skirt reaching midway between the knee and the ankles.

(S.No. 51 - M.No. 68-XXIV from Salar Jung Museum).

B. UN-SEWN CLOTH

Dupatta

Veil, the dupatta was also called 'Chunni', Odhni etc. This was used by the women to cover the head and bosom. (S.No. 32 - M.No. 59-XXV; S.No. 33 - M.No. 30-XXV; S.No. 34 - M.No. 191-XXV; S.No. 37 - M.No. 192-XXV; S.No. 38 - M.No. 88-XXV; S.No. 39 - M.No. 105-XXV; S.No. 69 - M.No. 213-XXV; S.No. 86 - M.No. 185-XXV; S.No. 87 - M.No. 195-XXV; S.No. 88 - M.No. 60-XXV; S.No. 89 - M.No. 181-XXV; S.No. 90 - M.No. 62-XXV; S.No. 91 - M.No. 65-XXV; S.No. 93 - M.No. 61-XXV; S.No. 94 - M.No. 182-XXV, from Salar Jung Museum and S.No. 20 - M.No. 8689 from State Museum).

Turban

The turban is an extremely important item of clothing. It protected the head from the sun and revealed at a glance the rank, religion and sometimes even the caste of a person, eg. The Rajputs and the men from Mysore in South India. The '*Chakridar*' was a '*Turban*' used by Muslims of Mysore. The Turban in its unfolded condition was 9 to 12 inches in width and 15 to 25 yards in length. (S.No. 53 - M.No. 25-XXV from Salar Jung Museum and State Museum S.No. 69 - M.No. 5273).

Patka

Girdle or a cloth for the loins into which the ceremonial sword was slipped. (S.No. 70 - M.No. 174-XXV; S.No. 71 - M.No. 179-XXV; S.No. 72 - M.No. 125-XXV; S.No. 80 - M.No. 3-XXV; S.No. 103 - M.No. 79-48; S.No. 105 - M.No. 65-XXIV; S.No. 107 - M.No. 83-XXIV *Patkas* from State Museum include S.No. 14 - M.No. 2599 and S.No. 15 - M.No. 2600).

Kamarbandh

A shawl or scarf which was bound round the waist; waist-band (S.No. 79 - M.No. 58-XXV from Salar Jung Museum).

Saris

A traditional wear of the majority of Indian women. The length of the sari vary from 5 metres to 8.2 metres, depending on the fashion and style of wear. Sari is worn over a petticoat, and choli or a blouse. (S.No. 23 - M.No. 62-18; S.No. 24 - M.No. 62-38-1; S.No. 25 - M.No. 67-XXV; S.No. 26 - M.No. 77-XXV; S.No. 28 - M.No. 79-XXV; S.No. 29 - M.No. 76-XXV; S.No. 30 - M.No. 64-XXV; S.No. 31 - M.No. 80-41; S.No. 35 - M.No. 80-42; S.No. 36 - M.No. 80-40; S.No. 74 - M.No. 75-XXV; S.No. 77 - M.No. 64-56; Saris from State Museum, S.No. 16 - M.No. 2605; S.No. 38 - M.No. 6488).

Shawls

Also known as '*Chadars*' It is used as a protective cover to the body from cold during winter season. There are several varieties of shawls. But the Pashmina Shawls of

Kashmir are the most famous ones. (S.No. 11 - M.No. 55-XXV; S.No. 12 - M.No. 50-XXV; S.No. 13 - M.No. 62-15; S.No. 14 - M.No. 424-XLIV; S.No. 17 - M.No. 46-XXV; S.No. 18 - M.No. 48-XXV; S.No. 19 - M.No. 40-XXV; S.No. 20 - M.No. 43-XXV; S.No. 22 - M.No. 51-XXV; S.No. 47 - M.No. 40-XXIV; S.No. 48 - M.No. 42-XXV from Salar Jung Museum and State Museum, M.No. 929; S.No. 33 - M.No. 5276).

C. FURNISHING FABRICS

Tapestry

An ornamental textile used for decorations; also used as curtains. (S.No. 28 - M.No. 8755; S.No. 29 - M.No. 7107 of the State Museum, Hyderabad).

Bed Covers & Bed-Sheets

A sheet; Bed spread. (S.No. 46 - M.No.1050-51 from State Museum, Hyderabad).

(S.No. 15 - M.No. 53-XLII; S.No. 16 - M.No. 64-47; S.No. 27 - M.No. 154-XXV from Salar Jung Museum and (S.No. 61 - M.No. 1027, State Museum, Hyderabad).

Palanquin Covers

Palki covers, cloth used to cover the palanquins. (S.No. 54 - M.No. 2-XXIV from Salar Jung Museum).

Tray Cover

Small pieces of cloths sometimes round or rectangular in shape to cover trays. (S.No. 57 - M.No. 56-XXIV; S.No. 81 - M.No. 46/2-XXIV from Salar Jung Museum).

Dastarkhan

Printed red or white cloth on which dishes are served on festivals and occasions. It is used mostly in Muslim homes. This item is available with State Museum, Hyderabad (S.No. 49 - M.No. 3697).

Masnads

Couch Covers (S.No. 57 - M.No. 56-XXIV from the Salar Jung Museum).

Ja-Namaz

Prayer mats-oblong cloth used by Muslims for sitting and standing on while offering of prayers. (State Museum, Hyderabad S.No. 50 - M.No. 3698).

Pichchwai

Backdrop behind the deity in Temples; (S.No. 50 - M.No. 79-40; S.No. 98 - M.No. 63-85; S.No. 109 - M.No. 80-39; S.No. 117 - M.No. 19-XLII; S.No. 118 - M.No. 74-67 from the Salar Jung Museum. Two Pichchwais from the State Museum are also included in the study. They are : S.No. 51 - M.No. 87-44; S.No. 72 - M.No. 6788).

Patachitras/Curtains

Temple hangings depicting legends from Hindu Mythology. (S.No. 97 - M.No. 63-60; S.No. 112 - M.No. 73-87; S.No. 113 - M.No. 87-9 from Salar Jung Museum). (The State Museum, Hyderabad. S.No. 64 - M.No. 2000; S.No. 21 - M.No. 80-

18 and 19; S.No. 73 - M.No. 6791; S.No. 71 - M.No. 6782. These fall under the category of *patachitras*. There are some good specimens of curtains in the two Museums under study. Salar Jung Museum - S.No. 21 - M.No. 21-XXIII; S.No. 41 - M.No. 65-XLII; S.No. 42 - M.No. 1-XXII; S.No. 49 - M.No. 79-39; S.No. 96 - M.No. 7-XXII; S.No. 99 - M.No. 24-XL; S.No. 110 - M.No. 216-CSI; S.No. 111; S.No. 116 - M.No. 62-51; S.No. 119 - M.No. 215-CSI; S.No. 120 - M.No. 63-55. State Museum, Hyderabad, S.No. 47 - M.No. 2353 and S.No. 68 - M.No. 3449).

D. MIXED FABRICS

The following ornamental textiles are used for different purposes as decorative specimens and are also used for making different costumes.

Himroo

A fabric of intricate weave. It is a fabric with cotton warp and silk or artificial silk or rayon weft. It was used for making tunics, bodices etc. It is now being used as tapestry material in luxury hotels, Embassies, Government Buildings etc. It is also used as a shawl. (Salar Jung Museum - S.No. 4 - M.No. 6-XXV; S.No. 40 - M.No. 62-26; S.No. 45 - M.No. 62-31-4; S.No. 66 - M.No. 106-XXV; S.No. 68 - M.No. 172-XXV; S.No. 82 - M.No. 131-XXV).

Mashru

Basically a pure silk cloth with designing done in zari work. The cloth was mainly used for wedding sherwani and for pyjamas of ladies.

Kimkhabs

It is an interweaving of silk and gold threads in a rich variety of colours and floral designs. It is used for making dresses for both ladies and gents. (S.No. 2 - M.No. 94-XXV; S.No. 6 - M.No. 108-XXV; S.No. 64 - M.No. 87-XXIV; S.No. 83 - M.No. 91-XXV, from Salar Jung Museum).

Jamdanis

The figured muslins of Bengal are known as Jamdanis. They were also used as Saris. (Salar Jung Museum - S.No. 78 - M.No. 24-XXV; S.No. 104 - M.No. 53-XXIV).

The needle and sewing are mentioned in the *Rig Veda* and the *Amara Sinha*. The *Amara Sinha* mentions two words for workers with needles, one applying exclusively to darners and the other to general tailoring. The first is *tunnavaya*, a word similar to *tantuvaya*, a weaver, and the other *sauchika* or *suchika- a* general worker with needle. The sculptures of Sanchi, Barhut, Amaravati and Orissa show made up dresses although the majority of figures are shown in the nude. In Sanchi bas-reliefs the figures are shown wearing tunics.[1]

In Orissa, in the queen's palace among the rock-cut caves of Udayagiri a statue is seen dressed in a close fitting tunic *(Chapkan)* with skirts hanging 4 inches below the knees and with sleeves hanging down to the wrists. A light scarf passes round the waist and over the left shoulder, the ends floating in the air. A *Kummerband* - like girdle round the waist holds, on the left side, a sword.[2]

The forms of ancient made-up garments having fallen into disuse, their names have also now become obsolete. For example, *Kancholika, Angika, Chola, Kurpasaka* etc., of these the *Kancholika* that is a jacket or a coat is defined as a soldier's dress in the form of bodice hanging either upto the hip or down to the leg.

The *Mahabharata* describes the sages and hermits who attended the great festival of Yudhishthira as being dressed in *Turbans* and *Kancukas*.

In the *Ratnavali*- Sriharsha gives a picture of warder who offers protection to a dwarf under the folds of the *Kanchuka* when he was frightened by a monkey.

The *Kanchuka* or the *Kanchulika* is a cloth bodice worn by highly placed women and Goddesses. Till the beginning of the twentieth century, a thin light jacket reaching the waist with elbow length sleeves, was worn over the *Kanchulika* and was known as the *Angia*. The name of the male jacket may be corruption of the same word *Angarkha*.[3]

The Use of veil, bodice, and body clothes are repeatedly mentioned in the *Ramayana* and *Mahabharata*. The Veil, as a mark of propriety and respect before elders and strangers, is everywhere insisted upon. Even for men a single garment is forbidden.[4]

The *Upanishads* also state that two pieces were worn both by the males and females, the uttariya or upper garment and *antariya* or lower garment. The *Turban* or the ceremonial head-dress was in fashion and a local custom of the period. The turban was worn by both male and female.

The Vedic and Epic Ages have mentioned about textiles but there is no sculptural description. We get only words used for dresses but there is not a single description regarding the nature and mode of wear.

For the first time in Indian history at the beginning of the 2nd century B.C., we come across sculptures displaying the costumes of the day. These are the *yaksha* statues from Parkhan and Baroda now in possession of the Mathura Museum. The dress of the Parkhan figure comprises of a dhoti like lower garment reaching down to the ankles. This garment is adorned with a *Patka* which is a narrow band of embroidered cloth with ornamental fringes. The *patka* not only serves the purpose of decoration but also provides a proper cover between the two legs. A *Kamarbandh* is fastened over the garment with a knot, the two ends of which hang upto the knees.

The Didarganj Yakshini, portrays the female costume, a lower garment reaching down the ankles. The Yakshini is also seen wearing a *Patka* and a scarf tucked in the girdle. Though there is a controversy about dating of these figures, however, they are placed somewhere near the close of the Mauryan period of the beginning of the Sunga dynasty. From then onwards it took almost a century to detect any changes in the style of dress. Thus, it can be assumed that the people dressed themselves in a similar manner as depicted in these sculptures even during Asoka's time.[5] That the fashion of wearing coat was in practice is also indicated by terracotta figurines of Sunga Period found at different sites. A figure of man found at Bhita wears a sleeved coat like the modern *Choga* which is open but provided with loop and knot to fasten it across the chest. On the railing of stupa II at Sanchi represents a soldier wearing a half-sleeved *Kurta (Tunic)* reaching to the knees fastened round the waist with a *Kamarbandh*.[6]

The heads of women in Barhut sculptures are always seen covered with beautiful *Veils*. At places women are also represented wearing *Dupatta.* Though the turban is specially used by men, women also used it.[7]

The main article of dress of the male figures during the Satavahana period continued to be a *Dhoti* fastened by a *Kamarbandh,* and a twisted scarf. All the male figures are seen wearing a *Turban,* in different fashions or styles. The women of this age are represented with a lower garment worn in two different fashions. The heads of women are generally covered with *Odhinis* decorated with beautiful borders. These odhnis were worn in different styles. *Turbans* are also sometimes worn by the women.

The Sanchi sculptures also represent some sewn garments, worn by charioteers, soldiers, foreigners etc. The chief garment represented in these sculptures is a *Tunic* sometimes with full sleeves and sometimes quarter-sleeved, fastened at the waist by a *Kamarbandh* and a *Scarf* streaming at the back.[8]

The first three hundred years of the Christian era provide ample material to reconstruct the history of Indian costume through the sculptures of Gandhara, and Mathura in the North, and the reliefs of Amaravati, Nagarjunakonda, etc., in the South.

During this period we find a slight change in the wearing of the *Kamarbandh.* The Kushana sculptures from Mathura, Gandhara Sculptures from the then North-Western India and reliefs from Amaravati and Nagarjunakonda provide us with a new fashion of wearing the *Kamarbandh* and the *Turban.* The old ribbon-like *Kamarbandh* developed into a boarder one which was displayed by both men and women in various styles. But in the male costume, the turban with an upward turret-like projection became the fashion. Dress habits of the North and South of India continued to be identical.[9]

The *Kamarbandh* disappeared from the scene during the third century A.D. The *Sari* or lower garment of the women was of a longer length. The scarf of the earlier century was replaced by a board cloth, or a *Shawl,* which was thrown across the shoulder. There were a variety of styles to wear the *Chadar.* On some occasions the long shawl was used by women as cover from head to foot, serving even for a veil.[10]

For the costumes of the fourth century, interestingly, many Gupta coins show the emperors wearing a light-fitting half-sleeved *Tunic* with two pointed lower ends projecting on the sides and tight fitting trousers of a *Chudidar* type. Sometimes the tunic had a coat-like open front with buttons and fasteners. Women continued to wear the lower garment upto the knees in the Maharashtrian style secured with a light *Kamarbandh* at the waist.[11]

Several garments were extensively used. One more interesting information from this period available is that the appearance of different patterns on the materials out of which the clothes were fashioned. At Ajanta we find representations of *Pillows, Curains* and *Cushions* with textile designs. In Cave XVII a glimpse of two *Curtains* is obtained. One is of a dark green colour divided into panels by dotted lines with white flowers appearing on the surface. The second curtain bears ochre-coloured stripes with bluish flower petals appearing on white ground. In Cave XVII a *Cushion* made of striped material is seen.

The famous Benaras *Kimkhobs* are represented in Cave XVII used as back curtains.[12]

It is also interesting to note that during the period from the third century A.D. to the end of the seventh century, all the chief fabric materials studied in this work are represented through one source or the other-literature and art. They also include the various designs and colours, the chief sewn and unsewn textiles under study in the present chapter.

The sartorial styles of the previous centuries continued with minor regional deflections during the eight to the twelfth century in the history of Indian costumes and textiles. We see people wearing bright coloured garments. Heun-Tsang records that men wore *Caps* on their heads.[13] The men continued with their *Dhoti*, the *Patkas*, the ornamented *Kamarbandhs* and the sewn garments. The women wore a *Bodice*, the *Sari* or an undergarment. The women of Kashmir are said to have worn the *Shawls* of goat-hair.[14]

During the era of the Sultans and the Mughal Emperors, the conquerors wore tight-fitting trousers, a *Light-sleeved Long Coat* fitting up to the waist before flaring out in a full skirt, and a closely tied *Turban*. The dress of their women was like that of Persian Princesses. But the conservative Indians were not prepared to copy the attire.[15] However, they worked out a solution to cover the bosom of their women, and the *Choli* was evolved.

Upto the time of Akbar, Persian dress was worn by Muslims but during Akbar's time Rajput dress was adopted. The Indian coat or *Angarkha,* fastened at the side as in China, was different from the Persian gown that buttoned down the front and fitted to the form. It may have been at this time that the veil, the *Dupatta* of the Rajput women, superceded the women's turban in the *zenana's* of the king and nobles and since then the skirt, bodice and veil of Rajasthan might have prevailed in the harems of the 17th century with constant changes of fashion. Abul Fazl, Akbar's friend and historian, gives a detailed account of the storing, manufacture and styles of dresses. According to the *Ain-i-Akbari*, Akbar took great interest in the conditions of work and produce of the workmen.[16]

Akbar affected changes of fashion by ordering court dress to be made with a round skirt and to be tied on the right side. He also introduced the fashion of wearing the shawl doubled *(Doshalla)*. Throughout the Mughal period, one of the most fancied articles of costume was a decorated patka into which the ceremonial sword was slipped. Golconda was the main centre specialising in the making of patkas.[17]

Under the Mughal patronage the textile industry saw great progress and till the end of the 18th century India could be described as one of the workshops of the world.

About the *Kashmir Shawls* Bernier writes, "The Mughals and Indians, women as well as men, wear them in winter round their heads, passing them over their left shoulder as a mantle. There are two sorts manufactured, one with the wool of the country finer and more delicate than that of Spain; the other kind with the hair found on the breast of a wild goat which inhabits the great Tibet."[18]

One of the most beautiful patterns in cotton evolved and perfected by the Muslims was *Jamdani*. The weaving of delicate flowers and leaves on the flimsiest cotton.[19] This is still produced at Tanda in the U.P. *Jamdanis* are also produced in Bengal. The figured Muslins of Bengal are known as *Jamdanis*. They are hand embroidered in the loom. Jamdanis are the most favourite possession of the women of Bengal and are worn at festive occasions.

Persian influence dominated in India too, and the tree of life pattern which became a favourite during this period was the mango design known in the west as the Paisley from shawls woven in that design in the island of that name. It was used for all conceivable patterns for corners, for over all decorations and for borders, and it came to be firmly associated with Muslim weaving. It adopted numerous forms, narrow, elongated, broad etc., are all popular even today.[20]

The use of material during this period was for making prayer mats *(Ja Namaz)* oblongs of cloth used by Muslims for sitting and standing on during the time of offering prayers. These were made of printed cotton, silk and woollen materials. The distinguishing feature was the design which distinguished it from small carpets. The archway of a mosque at one end and sometimes verses of the Quran woven in or printed.

Bernier also mentions *Wall Hangings*, some of brocaded velvet and others worked out in silks, silver, gilt and silver thread on a woven cotton ground. A good mixture of Persian and Indian influences, appear in these and some of them owed more to contemporary schools of Rajput painting than anything Persian.[21]

As the Mughal Empire decayed and many Hindu and Muslim kingdoms sprang up, the dress of the Muslims also underwent certain changes.

In the Muslim states of Bhopal and Hyderabad, the Mughal fashion continued with slight modifications. In Bhopal, the tight trousers came to be worn with a *Kurta* very like the Mughal tunic tight to the waist with a full skirt but here the skirt became shorter, reaching down a little above the ankles and the turban gave place to the *Dupatta*. In Hyderabad the women wore *Sarees*. Instead of the short blouse, they wore a long *Kurta* slit on both sides reaching below the knee. The men wore the tight trousers and *Angarkhas* of the Mughals, but later they wore a long loose robe fitting at the shoulder and open in front. This was known as the *Choga* and was generally worn by upper class men. The turban was replaced by different varieties of caps. But in the North-West provinces, the turban was still in use. It was also worn by the ruler and nobles on state occasions and the turban also formed an integral part of the dress of a bridegroom, as it does even to the present day. The old Mughal fashion persisted in the dresses of Muslim brides and bridegrooms.[22]

At what time during the Muslim period the saree was transformed from the Dhoti-like apparel of the Ajanta women into the present style, it is not possible to assert with certainty. But it may rightly be presumed that with the advent of the comparatively over dressed conquerors. The Hindu women also felt the need for a covering around the shoulders. One article of the attire of Muslim men which came into being during the latter part of the Muslim period was the *Achkan* which later came to be known as the *Sherwani*. This was the long coat reaching slightly below the knees, closing down the front. At the end of the nineteenth century and the Muslim men wore ornamental dresses which consisted of the churidar-pyjama of silk brocade, preferably *Mashroo* made in Hyderabad, with a *Muslin* tunic slit on both sides and reaching above the knees, and an ornate *Achkan* made of *Jamewar* was worn by the rich during the winter. During the summer light *Angarkhas* were worn.[23]

The modern century opened with a slight change in the dress that had prevailed earlier.

Western influence had pervaded the upper classes and professional and businessmen dressed in the approved Victorian style, with stiff collars, fully buttoned waistcoats, striped trousers etc. At home this dress was discarded and the *Kurta* and *Dhoti* or *Kurta* and *pyjamas* were worn. *Kurtas* were generally made of white muslin, embroidered or sometimes plain, but the *pyjamas* were made of heavy cotton brocades of Hyderabad, *mushroo* woven in Azamgarh and Bhopal and for the occasions the rich Benaras brocades.[24] The *Dupatta* still continued among the women of the upper classes. But in some regions of the country, the *Saree* was draped over the head and shoulders and a *Choli* became compulsory item of woman's dress. A petticoat also became an integral part of woman's dress. Though the traditional dhoti and saree were in vogue in most parts of India, the dresses in the South differed from the North. There were some Indians who took to the English costume.[25]

It may be mentioned here that the use of English dress was limited to a very small section of the population. A large population of Indians living mostly in the rural areas continued to use their own regional dress. In the following paragraphs, a brief narration of the contemporary dress of the South Indians with special reference to Andhra Pradesh is given. Ghurye has given us valuable information about the dress of the people living in the southern region of our country. This is an extract from his book.[26]

"The costume of the Andhras in the northern and eastern parts of Andhradesa reveals some affinities with the dress common in the Eastern region. The common features, along with some other peculiar to Andhradesa', will be met with in Tamilnadu. The male lower garment everywhere in the area among the respectable classes is of course the *Dhoti,* its standard length being not more than four yards. The simplest mode of wearing the garment is to wrap it round the loins holding it in position by the side tucks without any gathers or pleats either at the back or in front. When thus worn it hangs as a straight gatherless skirt like the *'ungi* and is known in Telugu as the *godakattu* manner of wearing the *Dhoti*. But this is not a very favourite mode here though in Tamilnad, it is the most frequent manner among the higher classes. The most common mode of wearing among the Andhras is called the *pancakattu* or *pancagattu* mode of wearing."

"The hind tucking is called *goci* in which one can see the reflection of the Kannada *kacce* or *gacce* which with its variant *kaccam* proclaims its origin to be Sanskritic. The front pleats are called *Kuccellu*. The other term for the same feature *madata* appears to be peculiar to Telugu. This mode of wearing is not only the routine manner with most of the people but is also good for formal or religious occasions with them, excepting only Brahmins and similar other classes. The latter, on occasions of ceremonial or ritual, have to put on their *dhoti* in the standard manner of the Brahmanic wear of that garment. For the upper part of the body a scarf was the much more general attire, and was almost an invariable component of the sartorial ensemble of the higher classes. It is known as *paibatta* and it is a prescribed item on ceremonial or religious occasions. In the matter of head dress the north-eastern part of Andhra approximates to the Eastern region in dispensing with a regular headgear but in the South-western part continuous with Karnataka the freshly folded attire, and was almost an invariable component of the sartorial ensemble of the higher classes. It is known as *paibatta* and it is a prescribed item on ceremonial or religious occasions. In the matter of head dress the north-eastern part of Andhra approximates to the Eastern region in dispensing with a regular headgear but in the south-western part continuous with Karnataka the freshly folded turban, generally white in colour tends to be more voluminous. The lower classes used a small piece of cloth to wind it round the head known as the *talapaga*".[27]

"The lower garment used by Andhra females is generally shorter than that favoured by Karnataka and Maharashtra women being either, rather than yards. It is called *cira* or *cire*. The standard mode of wearing it, current among non-Brahmanic groups, is known as *godakattu* a term which is also applied to the male lower garment when worn in the *lungi* fashion. But in the case of *sari* there are the front pleats which are either called *kuccellu* or *madata*. The portion of the *sari* to be drawn up over the upper part of the body is called *pamita* or *paita*.[28] Another mode of sari-wear common among the labouring classes is *mattagoci*. The mode is *godakattu*, a tucked-up wear and not a separate mode of putting on the sari. The front pleats of the *godakattu* mode are drawn up between the legs behind and tucked in at the back. Then the side-hangings of the sari are taken up and similarly tucked in at the sides.[29] In the *kasakattu* or *kasapuse* mode, the inner end of the left side portion of the sari is drawn up between the legs at the back and tucked in there. This is formal and ritual manner of sari-wear, which in the three Dravidian areas of Andhra, Karnataka and Tamilnad, is common among Brahmins. A bodice for the upper part of the body known as *ravika* is worn."[30]

Indian sartorial scenes have changed rather slowly. Certain basic fashions have remained the same for a long time. In fact any major change depends on the pressing demands of the times. Continuity and change are the two essential characteristics of a living culture. Culture assures that we are not totally uprooted from our past inheritance. The same phenomena applies to costumes as they represent one of the facets of a culture.

Referernces

1. Brij Bhushan, Jamila - Op.Cit., 1958, p.18.
2. Ibid, p.19.
3. Ibid, p.20.
4. Ibid., pp. 20-21.
5. Moti Chandra - Op.Cit., 1973, p.19.
6. Ibid.
7. Ibid, p.20.
8. Ibid, p.21.
9. Biswas, A. Op.Cit., 1985, pp.12-13.
10. Brij Bhushan, Jamila - Op.Cit., p.22.
11. Biswas, A. Op.Cit., 1985, pp.14-15.
12. Moti Chandra - Op.Cit., 1973, p.98.
13. Biswas, A. Op.Cit., 1985, pp.16.
14. Moti Chandra - Op.Cit., 1973, p.110.

15. Biswas, A. Op.Cit., 1985, pp.18.
16. Brij Bhushan, Jamila - Op.Cit., 1958, p.30.
17. Ibid, p.32.
18. Ibid, p.34.
19. Ibid, p.36.
20. Ibid., p.85.
21. Ibid, p.35.
22. Ibid, p.38.
23. Ibid, p.39.
24. Ibid, p.42.
25. Biswas, A. Op.Cit., 1985, pp.30.
26. Ghurya, G.S. Op.Cit., 1951, pp.204-207.
27. Ibid, p.205.
28. Ibid.
29. Ibid., p.206.
30. Ibid, p.207.

CHAPTER - VII

STORAGE AND PRESERVATION

In the Museums, one can find on display and in storage, fabrics and costumes of cotton, silk, wool and mixed fibres, embroidered, dyed or painted, brocaded and so on. Sometimes, on one textile may be found a blend of different techniques. Dresses of different shapes and sizes are also available. Furthermore, textile fibres being of a very delicate nature, the fabrics are almost always in a weak and fragile condition. The range of textiles in the possession of the museums is so wide that different types of preservation problems arise. Textiles being organic in nature and made of delicate fibres are susceptible to various types of deterioration factors like humidity, light, micro-organisms, insects etc.

The life of a fabric depends on two fundamental factors:[1]

1. The nature and quality of the fabric, the manufacturing process, the colours used and the nature of the fibres
2. The agents of deterioration to which it is subjected like environment, light, storage conditions, handling and so on.

All these factors combined together work on textiles to damage them.

Humidity

It is significant that, in India very few fabrics of a period earlier than the seventeenth century are now available. The reason is the hot and humid conditions prevailing in our country. Humid climate is probably the greatest enemy of textiles. Constant climatic conditions are conducive to the preservation of all types of organic material. The acceptable range for textiles, is relative humidity 45% to 55% and temperature between 55^0 to 68^0 F. This atmosphere has to be maintained at the specific level throughout the year, day and night. This standard can be brought about only by air-conditioning, which is not possible for large museums. However, a limited control can be achieved by suitable orientation of the building, shading of windows, devising of show-cases etc.

Light

With the effect of light, the fabrics are weakened and its colours get faded. It has been found that natural sunlight direct or indirect has more ultra-violet rays and infra-red rays than florescent tubes or bulbs have. The ultra-violet rays which are contained in light are mostly responsible for affecting textiles because they are of short wave length and contain high energy. Dyes fade principally due to the effect of visible portion of light. Hence, care must be taken to protect the textiles from being damaged by the ill-effects of the light. The intensity of light in the galleries or wherever the textiles are displayed or stored should be kept low. A level of 50 lux is recommended for this purpose. The ultra-violet portion of the light may be filtered with the help of the ultra-violet absorbing filters. In the textile galleries light should always be indirect, reflected against surface coated with chemicals like zinc oxide or titanium trioxide which have the capacity to absorb ultra-violet rays.[2]

Bio-Deterioration

Insects of various types like termites, cockroaches, wool-moths, beetles etc., and micro-organisms damage textiles in a big manner. Particular attention must be paid to protect textiles from insects. The first consideration is the periodic inspection of textile objects. Cleanliness of the exhibition galleries and storage rooms is quite necessary. For control of insects, insecticidal treatment is essential. A number of insecticides like DDT, Chlordane, Dieldrin, Pyrethrin, Paradichlorobenzene, Naphthalene balls and so on, have been recommended. Naphthalene balls however tend to tarnish brocade work on textiles. Brocaded textiles should not come in contact with naphthalene. All wooden shelves and cupboards should be coated with 1% solution of lindane. If by chance textiles get infected by insects they should be immediately isolated and fumigated in a laboratory. All types of textiles get fumigated in a laboratory.[3]

Textiles are also affected by fungus which weakens fabric and also stains them which is difficult to remove. Fungus grows quickly in humid climate, and textiles are particularly affected because all cellulosic material absorbs moisture from atmosphere and becomes potential seat for the growth of fungus[4]. To control this condition, good ventilation of storage areas and exhibition gallery are necessary. Some chemicals like Pentachlorophenol, Sodium Pentachlorophenate and others have been recommended as anti fungus. Periodical fumigation with Thymol vapours is also helpful.[5]

Storage and Handling

Textiles are very delicate and can be easily damaged if not handled and stored properly. When kept folded for a long time, they weaken at the folds and ultimately tear in those portions. The best way is to store them on rollers or tubes. The ends of the rollers should project beyond the textiles so that no folds are formed. The rollers are placed on hooks, fixed inside cupboards or they can be hung on frames. Frames are arranged in such a manner that they can slide on castors allowing a frame to be pulled out for the removal of the roller if the textile is required for study or display. When placing textiles on tubes, it should be ensured that creases do not creep in.[6] If folding of textiles cannot be avoided, folds should not be in a sharp crease, but should be padded with soft and clean tissue paper. The first fold should always be parallel to the warp. Warp strands are generally more strong because they are more lightly twisted than those of the weft, which are therefore more likely to be damaged by folding.[7]

Because costumes come in various shapes and sizes, they constitute a difficult problem of storage. They cannot be put on rollers or tubes. One method of storing them is to hang them on padded hangers, covered with polythene sheets or bags. Costumes on hangers are stored in a cabinet allowing ample space to avoid crushing. There is however a very great disadvantage in this method of storing costumes. The entire weight of the costumes falls on that part of the costumes which is supported by hanger. This type of strain on one particular part causes damage, weakening the fabric at that particular point. This strain can be avoided only if the costume is stored flat. Brocaded costumes are especially damaged by folding and need very careful padding.[8]

Drawers and cupboards for storing textiles should be constructed of wood and hard-board, both of which should be left unpolished.[9]

The cupboard should be made dust proof because dust is very destructive to textiles.

Because textile fibres are highly absorbant they become easily stained. Stains once caused are difficult to remove. They not only disfigure, but also damage the material of the textile. All precautions must be taken to ensure that textiles are always kept on tables which are covered with cloth or polythene sheet. Textiles should not be touched with unclean hands. No food or drink, no ink or similar liquid, should be allowed in the storage area. Metal clips, pins or staples rust very quickly and should not be used on textiles otherwise they will leave stains. This practice is dangerous, because it not only damages the textiles but also leaves a stain. For giving identification numbers, it is best to write them on cloth tapes which are then stitched on to the textiles with needle and thread.[10]

Mentioned above are only the fundamental principles of textiles preservation. If attention is paid to protect them from the ill-effects of various factors of damage, if timely action is taken to wash them and reinforce them; if precautions are taken that they are stored and handled properly, the process of their deterioration can be slowed down, if not halted altogether.[11]

As mentioned earlier, there are nearly 20 Tibetan ***Thangkas*** in possession of the State Museum, Hyderabad. The Thangkas are holy banners of the Tibetans. They are in various sizes, hanging from a stick on which they can be rolled up, and covered by a thin silk. A Thangka has in its centre a painting, always vertical in format. It has a mounted silk border stitched all around, with two sticks, one on top and the other at the bottom, which is heavier than the upper one and acts as a weight to hang the Thangka straight. A string is attached to the two ends of the top stick, by which it is hung on a wall or on a pole. When storing, the Thangka is rolled up on the rod.

Preservation of Old Thangkas present some peculiar problems. Because there is a difference in the structure and construction of the painting and of the border, the two have to be separated and treated separately. The central part of the Thangka i.e., the painting part has to be treated like a painted surface. The borders can be repaired with needle and thread. If the painting is old and fragile, it needs to be lined with fresh material. While selecting the technique of lining of thangka, it is to be kept in mind that the Thangka was meant for rolling. The whole assembly after lining should not become rigid.[12]

Thus, precautions must be taken to handle textiles very carefully when they are on display or in the stores. Timely treatment of the brittle and fragile fabrics not only helps to improve its appearances but also prolongs its life.

References

1. Marg Publications - *Treasures of Indian Textiles,* Bombay, 1980, p.140.
2. *Purabhilekha-Puratattva* Vol.IX, Number I, 1991, p.72.
3. Ibid., p.74.
4. Ibid., p.72.
5. Marg Publications, *Op.Cit.,* 1980, p.141.
6. Ibid., p.142.
7. Purabhilekha-Puratattva, *Op.Cit.,* 1991, p.74.
8. Ibid., p.77.
9. Marg Publications, *Op.Cit.,* 1980, p.142.
10. Ibid.
11. Ibid.
12. Leene, J.E. (Ed.) - *Textile Conservation,* London, 1972, p.226.

BIBLIOGRAPHY

ORIGINAL SOURCES

1. Textiles on Display in the Salar Jung Museum and
2. Textiles in the Stores of the State Museum, Hyderabad

MODERN WORKS

A. Books

Agrawal	*Museum Studies,* Varanasi, 1973.
Alexandra Trone (Translated)	*Conservation and Restoration of Works of Art and Antiquities,* London, 1986.
Angus Geijar	*A History of Textile Art,* London, 1979.
Barua, B.K.	*A Cultural History of Assam,* Vol.I Gauhati, Assam, 1969.
Biswas, A.	*Indian Costumes,* New Delhi, 1985.
Brij Bhushan Jamila	*The Costumes and Textiles of India,* Bombay, 1958.
Dhamija, Jasleen	*Indian Folk Arts and Crafts,* New Delhi, 1970.
Dongerkery S. Kamala	*The Romance of Indian Embroidery,* Bombay, 1951.
Dwivedi, V.P. (Ed)	*Museums and Museology,* New Horizons, Delhi, 1980.
Fabri, Charles	*Indian Dress,* New Delhi, 1977.
George Watts & Percy Brown	*Arts and Crafts of India,* New Delhi, 1979.
George Watt (Ed)	*Indian Art at Delhi,* Calcutta, 1903.
Ghurye, G.S.	*Indian Costume,* Bombay, 1951.
Griswold, Lester	*Handicraft simplified procedure and projects.*
Hadway, W.S.	*Cotton Painting and Printing in Madras Presidency,* Madras, 1917.
Havel, E.B.	*Handloom Weaving in India,* 1905.
Jasleen Dhamija & Jyotindra Jain (Eds)	*Handloom Fabrics of India.*
Jayakar, P (Ed)	*Textiles and Ornaments of India,* Newyork, 1956.
Kamaladevi Chattopadhyay	*Indian Handicrafts,* Delhi, 1963.
Kameswara Rao, V.	*Select Vijaynagar Temples of Rayalaseema,* Hyderabad, 1976.
Krishna Murthy, K.	(1) *Nagarjunakonda, A Cultural Study,* Delhi, 1977.

	(2) *Nolamba Sculptures - A Cultural Study,* Delhi, 1987.
	(3) *Mirrors of Indian Culture,* New Delhi, 1982.
Leena, J.E.	*Textile Conservation,* London, 1972.
Majumdar, R.C. (Ed)	*The History and Culture of Indian People,* Vol.I, London, 1951.
Margabandhu C.	*Archaeology of the Satavahana Kshatrapa Times,* Delhi, 1985.
Mc Crindle, J.W.	*Ancient India as described by Megasthanese and Arrian,* Calcutta, 1926.
Mehta, Rustom, J.	*The Handicrafts and Industrial Arts of India,* Bombay, 1960.
Moreland	*From Akbar to Aurangzeb,* London, 1920.
Motichandra	*Costumes, Textiles, Cosmetics and Coiffure in Ancient and Medieval India,* Delhi, 1973.
Mukherjee, A.K.	*Textile India,* Calcutta, 1956.
Nigam, M.L.	(1) *Sculptural Heritage of Andhra Desa,* Delhi, 1980.
	(2) *Decorative Arts of India,* Hyderabad, 1981.
Pratapaditya Pal and Hsien-ch'I Tseng	*Lamaist Art,* Boston
Rajendra Prasad, B.	*Art of South India,* Andhra Pradesh, Delhi, 1980.
Ramanaiah, J.	*Temples of South India,* New Delhi, 1989.
Rama Rao M.	*Select Andhra Temples,* Hyderabad, 1970.
Raza Ali Khan	*Hyderabad 400 years* (1591-1991) Hyderabad, 1990.
Robinson, Russel H.	*Arms and Armour Series,* London, 1967.
Sachidanand Sahay	*Indian Costumes, Coiffure and Ornament,* New Delhi, 1975.
Saraswati, S.K.	*Indian Textiles,* Faridabad, 1961.
Schoff (Ed)	*The Periplus of the Erythrean Sea*, New Delhi, 1974.
Shama Shastry, R (Ed)	*Arthasastra* (Translated) Mysore, 1951.
Singh A.P.	*Conservation of Museum Techniques,* Delhi 1987.
Sivarama Murthy, C.	(1) *The Vijayanagara Paintings,* Delhi, 1985.
	(2) *Amaravati Sculpture in the Madras Government Museum,* Madras, 1977.
Solvyns, B	*Costume of Indostan,* London, 1977.
Sreepadma, B	*Costume, Coiffure and Ornaments in the Temple Sculpture of Northern Andhra,* Delhi, 1991.
Subrahmanyam, B	*Pre, Proto and Early Historic Cultures in Krishna-Tungabhadra Valley,* Delhi, 1997.
Uma Maheswari, C.S.	*Dress and Jewellery of Women,* Madras, 1995.
Venkateshwara Rao, A.	*Handloom Industry of India - A Study,* New Delhi, 1973.

Warmington — *Commerce between the Roman Empire and India,* 1974.
Zaheer, M. — *Museum Managements,* Lucknow, 1963.
Zwalf, W (Ed) — *Buddhism, Art and Faith,* London, 1986.

B. Journals and Bulletins

Mulk Raj Anand (Ed) — *Marg Publication,* "Textiles and Embroideries of India" Bombay, New Delhi.
(1) Article - "Looms" by DSV Iyer, pp.56-62.
(2) Article - "Telia Rumals of Pochampalli and Chirala" by Jagadish Mittal, pp.26-28.

Pupul Jayakar (Ed) — Section - II "Embroideries"
(1) Article - "Origin and Development of Embroidery in our Land" by Kamaladevi Chattopadhyaya, pp.5-10.

Kamala S. Dongerkery — "The Romance of Indian Embroidery", Bombay, 1951.
Article - "Phulkari of the Punjab", pp.25-28.

Mulk Raj Anand — *Marg Publications,* "Homage to Kalamkari", Bombay Vol.XXXI.
(1) Article - "Towards a Definition of Kalamkari" by Lotika Varadarajan, pp.19-22.
(2) Article - "Gaiety in Colour and Form", p.23.
Marg Publications, "Treasures of Indian Textiles", Bombay, 1980.
Article - "Conservation of Textiles" by O.P. Agarwal, pp.135-142.
Marg Publications, "Textiles in Historical Perspective" by John Irwin, p.4.

Andhra Pradesh Journal of Archaeology, Vol.I, 1979.
Bharatiya Vidya Journal, Vol.I, Part II.
Bi-Annual Research Journal, Salar Jung Museum, Hyderabad.
Bulletin Madras Government Museum, Vol.I, Part I.
Bulletin Madras Government Museum, Vol.IV, 1942.
Hyderabad Art and Archaeology and Handicraft, Delhi, 1952.
Itihas, Vol.3, No.1, Hyderabad, 1980.
Journal of Bihar and Orissa Research Society, March, 1932, Vol.XVIII - Part I and Vol.XX.
Journal of Indian Museum, Vol.XXXVII, New Delhi, 1981.
Lalit Kala, No.5, 1969.

C. CENSUS

Census of India, 1961, Vol.II, Part VII - A(1)
Census of India, 1961, Vol.II, Part VII - A(2)

Census of India, 1961, Vol.IX, Part VII - A(1)
Census of India, 1961, Vol.XI, Part VII - A(3)
Census of India.

D. Gazetteers

The Imperial Gazetteer of India, Vol.III, 1908.
The Imperial Gazetteer of India, Provincial Services, 1908.

E. Dictionaries and Encyclopaedia

John Richardson - *Dictionary* - Persian, Arabic and English, p.737 and p.849.
The New Encyclopaedia Britannica Marcopaedia, Vol.18, 15th Edition, Chicago, 1981, p.177.

PLATE

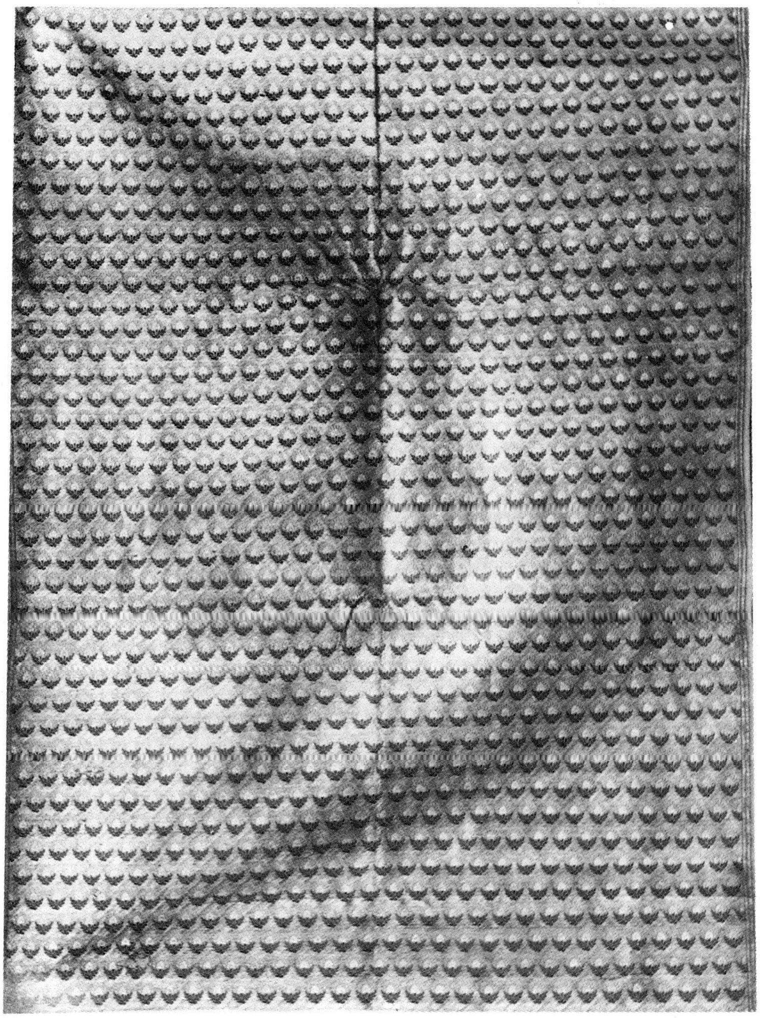

PLATE 1. 94-XXV - KIMKHOB

PLATE 2. 62-84 - SHERWANI

PLATE 3. 84-XXIV - CHOWBAGHLA

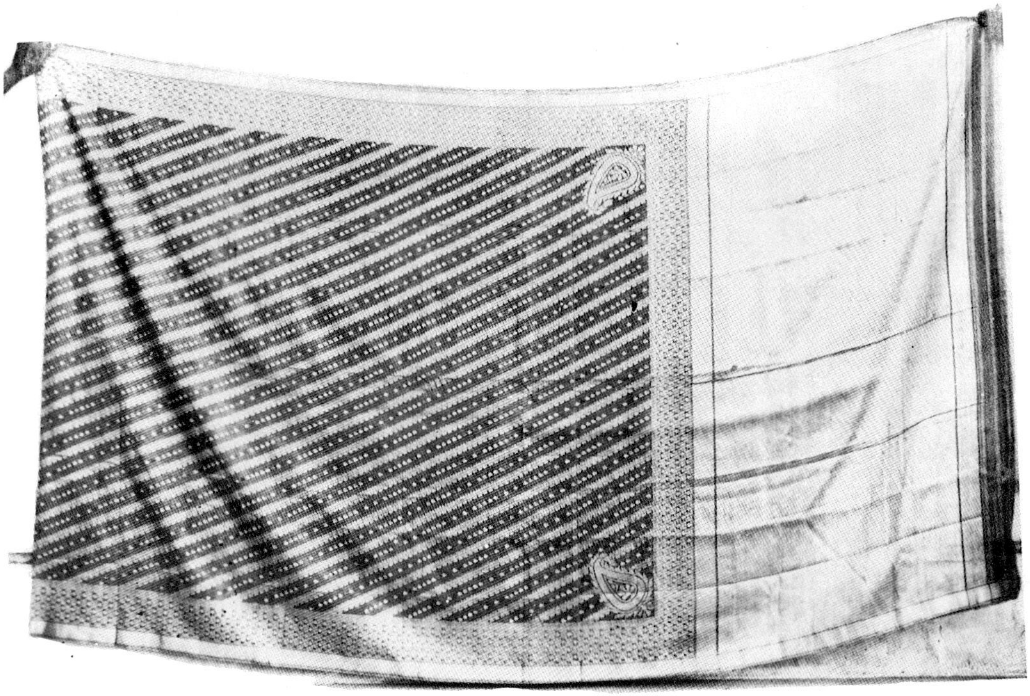

PLATE 4. 80-42 BENARAS BROCADE SAREE

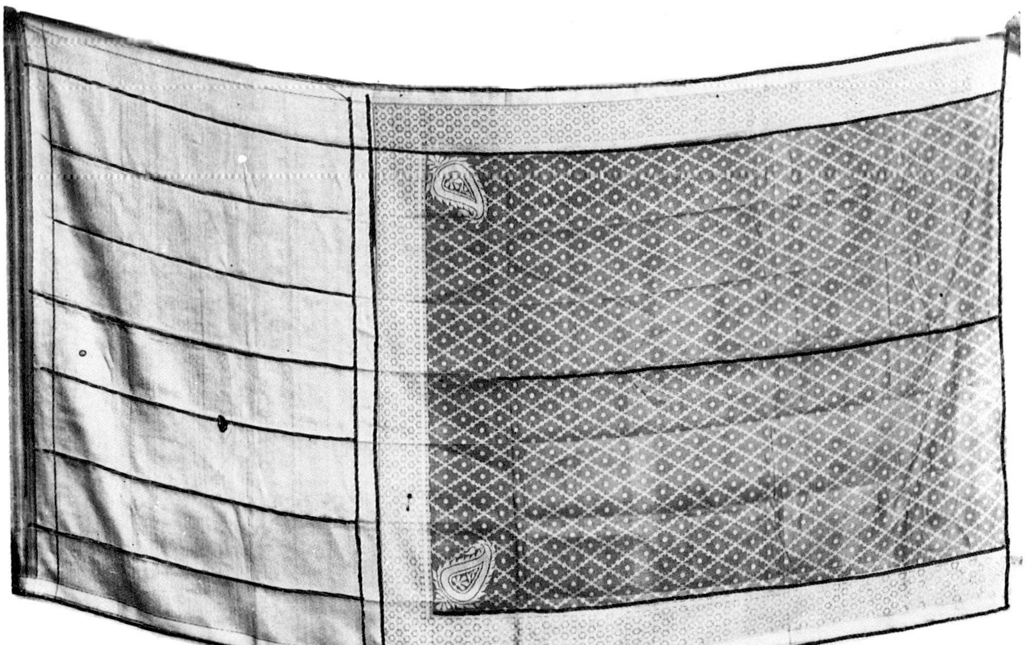

PLATE 5. 80-40 BENARAS SARI - DIAMOND DESIGN

PLATE 6. 72-26 CHOGA - AURANGABAD - STRIPPED PATTERN

PLATE 7. 79-39 SILK PICHCHWAI - SHIKARGA SCENE

PLATE 8. 79-40 COTTON - PICHCHWAI

PLATE 9. 68-XXIV MIXED FABRIC - BENARAS KURTA

PLATE 10. 63-60 COTTON - PATACHITRA RAJASTHAN PLATE 11. 53-XXIV COTTON (MUSLIN) - JAMDANI AND PATKA

PLATE 12. 216-CSI COTTON - KALAMKARI CURTAIN

PLATE 13. 63-55 COTTON - KALAMKARI CURTAIN

PLATE 14. RESERVE COLLECTION - BENARAS KURTA/ANGARKHA

PLATE 15. 2354 KALAMKARI SCREEN-CURTAIN (GAJENDRA MOKSHAM) SCANE

3691 MUSLIN CHINTZ CURTAIN

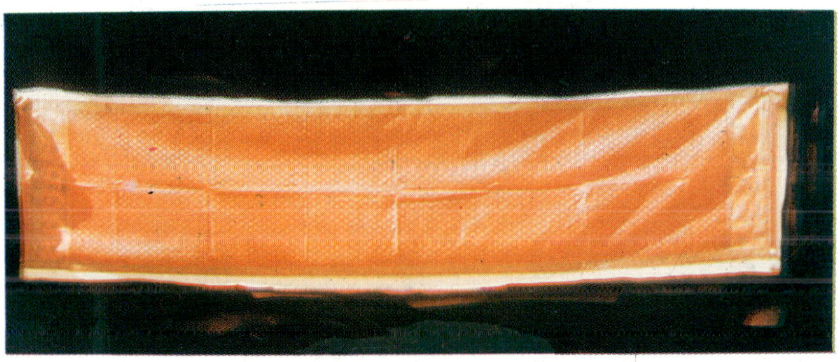

2600 SILK PATKA

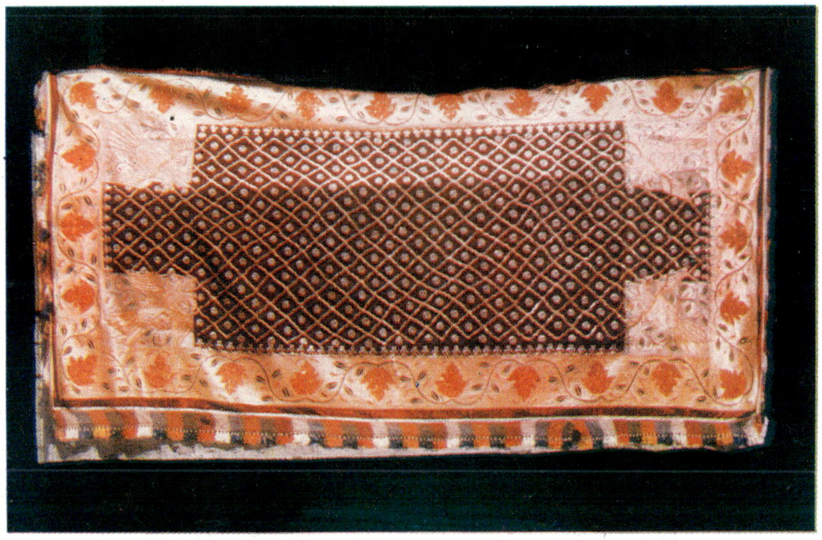

7107 SILK TAPESTRY-WALL-HANGING

1032 COTTON CLOTH - LAHORE PRINT

1035 COTTON CLOTH - LAHORE PRINT

1042 COTTON CLOTH - RUMAL - LAHORE PRINT

2354 COTTON KALAMKARI SCREEN-CURTAIN

8744 COTTON KALAMKARI WALL-HANGING

5613 COTTON PHULKARI - PUNJAB

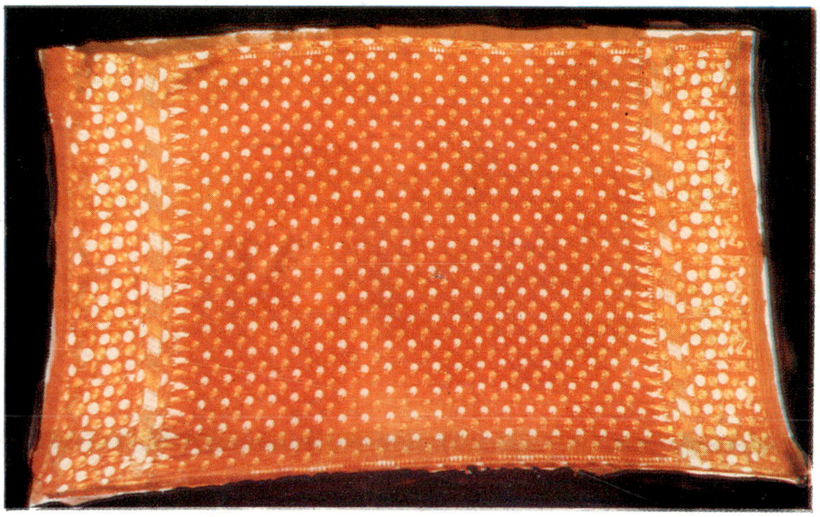

6490 COTTON PHULKARI - PUNJAB

4779 ASAFIA FLAG

2571 A - SILK JAMEWAR

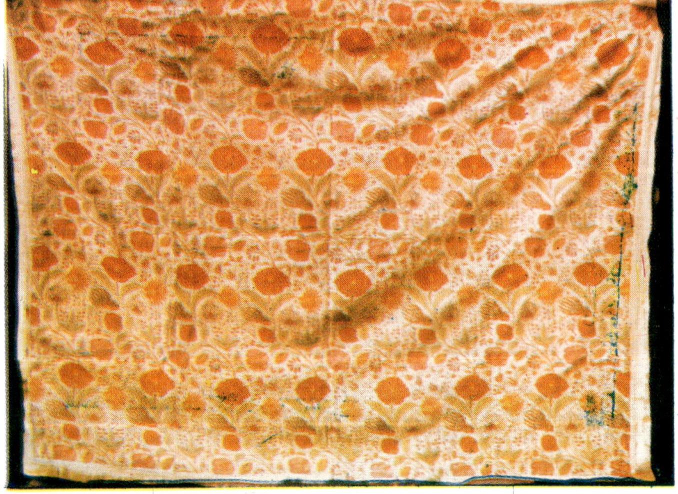

SILK JAMEWAR

JANAMZ SOURCE : HOMAGE TO KALAMKARI

JANAMZ SOURCE : HOMAGE TO KALAMKARI

ASAFIA FLAG SOURCE : 400 YEARS OF HYDERABAD

TIBETAN THANGKA, FRONT : SOURCE : TEXTILE CONSERVATION

TIBETAN THANGKA, BACK SOURCE : TEXTILE CONSERVATION

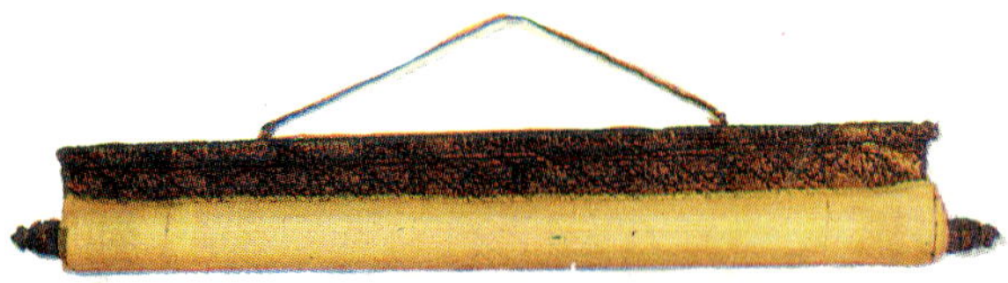

[illegible]

[illegible]